MAKING MUSIC IN TORBAY
Celebrating 140 Years

Malvern Cooke

Making Music in Torbay – Celebrating 140 Years

© Malvern Cooke

First Edition published 2012

Published by:
Palores Publications,
11a Penryn Street, Redruth, Kernow TR15 2SP, UK.

Designed & Printed by:
The St Ives Printing & Publishing Company,
High Street, St Ives, Cornwall TR26 1RS, UK.

ISBN 978-1-906845-35-3

MAKING MUSIC IN TORBAY

Celebrating 140 Years

Malvern Cooke
Honorary Secretary, South Devon Choir
1990 to date

An insight into the history, working
and management of a large
classical music choral society

PALORES
2012

Preface

THE FIRST PART of this history, particularly at the end of the 19th and early 20th century, has been based totally upon newspaper reports (except where a specific reference is mentioned). Unfortunately, no programmes, minutes or other Society records were available for this period at the time this history was written. They may well not exist at all. The amount of space given to the Paignton area and surrounds in Torquay-based newspapers was sparse. The main editorial column was followed by only two or three lines devoted to that part of the area. More local newspapers before March, 1877, are only held by the British Library, with no micro-film copies available in the Torquay Local History Reference Library. This obviously limits the author of this history to carry our further research about the Choir.

For the latter part of the nineteenth, and periods in the first half of the twentieth century, the fortunes of the Society are, to say the least, chequered! Starts and stops through lack of singers, particularly men, resulted in a lack of continuity of rehearsals and concerts. At some concerts, audiences were disappointing with the Society incurring financial losses. Because of these breaks in the activities and sparsity of information about the Society during them, additional music and relevant 'snippets' have been included. It is hoped the reader will find these of interest and even amusing!

Acknowledgments

NO AUTHOR CAN write a book without the valuable assistance of many people who provide background information and help with the compilation of the finished item. Considerable help and thanks are expressed to: Tony Moss of the Paignton Heritage Society (formerly Paignton Preservation Society); Frances Frith Collection for copyright permission to reproduce an old photograph of the Public Hall, Paignton; the Editor of the *Herald Express* for reproduction of photographs from past editions of the newspaper; Mike Thompson, our President, for old newspaper photographs of the Public Hall and Christ Church; Mark Pool and his colleagues in the Torquay Central Reference Library for using their expertise in providing answers to the many questions raised; past and present members of the Choir who have parted with cuttings, programmes and other keep-sake items which has helped build up the official history records; Sally and Brian Laird for meticulously proof-reading the text; John Christian for using his computer skills for work on the photographs and other pictorial images in this book; the publisher Les Merton, of Palores Publications, for his professional advice for my first venture in book publishing; finally my long suffering wife, Marsha, for my frequent disappearances upstairs on that "damned computer"!

Grateful thanks are expressed to The Co-operative Group which has kindly supported this project with a grant from the:

The **co-operative** membership community fund

My apologies for any remaining errors and to anyone else who I may have forgotten to thank.

Malvern Cooke

Every attempt has been made to ensure the accuracy of the information provided in this book at the time of writing, and the author regrets any discrepancies which subsequently may be identified.

Chapter 1
1873-1914

TO SET THE scene and background of the month in which it has been officially verified that the Paignton Choral Society was founded in 1871, the following are the facts of the time. Nationally, Queen Victoria was on the throne as Monarch and William Gladstone as Prime Minister. Locally, as reported in the 'Torquay Directory and South Devon Journal' produced each Wednesday at 2d (1p) per copy, the deposed Emperor, Charles Louis Napoleon (nephew of Napoleon Bonaparte I), with Empress Eugene and the Prince Imperial, had been recent visitors at the Imperial and Royal Hotels in Torquay, with the party attending Sunday Mass at the Church of the Ascension, Abbey Road, Torquay; Charles Hallé, famous for creating the Manchester based Hallé Orchestra and concerts, appeared in March at the Bath Saloon, Torquay, as guest pianist (this continued regularly throughout the 70's and 80's); Paignton had just two churches for worship – the parish church of St John the Baptist and an Independent Chapel (the Bible Christian Centre or Congregational Chapel now the Southfield Methodist Church); an Express train journey by 1st or 2nd class to London's Paddington Station averaged between seven and eight hours at a cost of £1.14.8 (£1.73); Paignton possessed two hotels – the Gerston (formerly on the site at the corner of Hyde Road and Torbay Road) advertising a double room for 3/6d per night (17½p) and a breakfast of cold meat or eggs 2/6d (12½p) for dinners from the same price and the other hotel, the Esplanade Hotel, Paignton Sands, advertising suites of apartments overlooking "Torquay, Berry Head and the Channel, good stabling and free use of Bathing Machines"; the Torquay Gas Company at their works in Hollacombe advertised coke at 14/- a ton (70p for just over 1,000 kg); eggs in the market were 1/10d a dozen (9p approximately for 12); pale ale was 1/6d for a gallon (7½p for 4½ litres); on a Monday and Tuesday in November eighty to one hundred thousand mackerel were caught with large quantities being given away; hackney carriages could be hired - for two passengers if drawn by a horse, 2/- (10p) for the first hour, but "if drawn by a man or a donkey, mule or other animal," 1/- (5p) per mile (just over 2.5 km); foot and mouth disease made its first appearance on a farm at Churston Ferrers. To draw a comparison with the prices quoted, a wage/salary for the following occupations at the time was: agricultural worker £41.1.0pa (£41.05); a teacher £97.0.1pa (£97); a domestic assistant £51.8.9pa (£51.44); engineer £94.7.7pa (£94.38); fisherman £66.4.0pa (£66.20).

We step back for the moment one year to 1870, when a wealthy Birmingham barrister, entrepreneur and Oxford graduate, Arthur Hyde Dendy, who had been called to the Inner Temple Bar in 1845, moved to Paignton. He was a patron of the arts, an accomplished musician and the proud possessor of a Stradivarius violin. He financed the building of the Gerston Hotel which opened in 1870 complete with the Bijou Theatre and livery stables. The latter was used for the hire of hearses and mourning coaches for funerals. Advertisements in the 'Torquay Directory' stated that the Theatre in the Hotel was entered by a separate staircase. In reality the only access was via a small doorway from the courtyard of the Hotel. It led to the "Gerston Saloon, Billiards and Supper Rooms, magnificently fitted up and brilliantly lighted. May be engaged for public and private Dinners, Parties. Concerts. Balls &c". The Manager was Mr Thomas Codner. A further article in the same paper mentioned the Bijou Theatre as luxurious and commented on the beauty of the décor and paintings. "The reserved seats consist of handsomely well-arranged stalls, in which the occupant may loll at his ease, enjoying at once all the amusements of a public performance with the comfort and luxury of a drawing room entertainment". Subsequent reports stated that the Theatre was "open all the year round. Its scenery is perfect and its performances are always good, no pains having been spared to make it a complete theatre . . . one of the most complete theatres out of London". In November, 1872, the title "Royal Bijou Theatre" suddenly appeared. As far as can be traced, this change does not appear to be attributed to any particular event, but in subsequent advertisements the word "Royal" was sometimes included, but usually dropped. As Mr Dendy was a controversial figure at times, did he ignore the fact that to use the title might have required royal assent? In 1873 more complimentary comments were made about the Theatre when the 'Torquay Directory' reported "Paignton can at length boast of being able to support a theatre. That delightful place of entertainment, the Bijou Theatre, has been in full swing for months past and there is no sign of diminished interest. People come in from the district around to visit it, from Totnes, Brixham and Torquay – it is no uncommon thing to see a long string of carriages waiting for their owners". Remaining until 1955/6, the Theatre, as part of the Gerston Hotel, occupied the site stretching from the corner of Hyde Road down to the site which Woolworths previously occupied and adjacent to the railway crossing. Space has been give to record information about the Royal Bijou Theatre, for, as we will see in a moment, the Paignton Choral Society gave two performances there and the Theatre achieved national fame, and still does, for a performance there in December, 1879.

So to the relevant facts about the Paignton Choral Society. The earliest reference to the Society has been traced to a minute dated 6 November, 1871, recorded by the Paignton Local Board of Health and now held in the Devon Record Office in Exeter stating "A letter received from Mrs Pridham asking leave to use the Town Hall for a Choral Society once a week". The Local Board of Health had five sub committees: Roads, Horse, Water, Building and Finance. The Clerk was directed to reply that the "Board will grant them use of the room once a week for the next six months at 5/- (25p) a night provided it be not on Mondays or Thursdays". Research to find out about Mrs Pridham and her interest in music revealed that she was Mrs Lucy Pridham, married to Dr Charles Pridham, MRCS, Admiralty surgeon and agent living at 1/2 Bishop's Place, Paignton. At the time of writing this book that address is still a Doctor's Surgery. The Pridhams appeared to have been held in high esteem in the community and they attended, or were involved in, many social events. Early in 1872, for example, their names appeared as guests at a New Year Opening Ball with an Italian Band playing, some days later at a Fancy Dress Ball and then a Masonic Grand Ball.

In 1878, it is noted that an article in the 'Paignton Gazette' reported that members of the Paignton Amateur Choral Society had come together to sing. However, no reports or concerts can be traced about the Society in any of the three main papers of the time, 'Paignton Gazette', 'Torquay Directory & South Devon Journal' or the 'Torquay Times & South Devon Advertiser' between November 1871 and April 1873. Further, at the General Meeting called in September of the latter year, it was resolved that the Society should lapse for one year (in fact this appears to have extended to four) so that membership might be increased. Part of this information appears to be corroborated by a newspaper article fifty years later. In 1924 Flaneur, the 'Paignton Observer & Echo' columnist, stated that a postcard dated 4 April, 1873, had been discovered in the possessions of the late Arthur Waycott. He was a local wine and spirit merchant whose business was founded in 1851 in Winner Street, Paignton, and organist until 1884 in the Parish Church and member of the local Masonic lodge. The postcard, originating from James Hunt, Secretary of the Choral Society, summoned Mr Waycott to a Committee Meeting in the Gerston Hotel Assembly Rooms (the Commercial Hotel by 1924) on 6 April, 1874, at 4 o'clock. Mr Hunt was aged twenty-three at the time and was ordained six years later as priest.

Before we take up the story of the Choral Society some other relevant events occurred and are recorded here in chronological order.

On the 27 October, 1875, the Memorial Stone of the New Congregational Church, Paignton, was laid by Mr Richard Southcombe of Stoke sub

Hamdon, Somerset. (Mr Southcombe was one of the founder members of the glove-making firm in that area which started in 1847 and still exists today.) The current site was described by one of the local newspapers of the time as "on the marsh abutting to the road leading to Brixham". The note of this event will have no relevance to this part of the Society's history for over one hundred years. The Church was later known as the Paignton United Reformed Church, and the adjacent hall in September, 1984, was to become the regular rehearsal hall for the Society. In 2006, with a diminishing congregation, the Church was closed and placed on the market for sale with the Choir having to find a new rehearsal place.

On 6 June, 1876, an Evening concert in aid of the Benevolent Funds and Charities of the Torbay Freemasons Lodge was held at the Bijou Theatre. Part I included a Festival Cantata composed by Mr Thomas Brooks who was organist, tutor and professor of music living in Paignton. A "full chorus of thirty voices" was advertised and may well have included members of the Paignton Amateur Choral Society which, at the time, appears to have been in abeyance or 'sleeping'. In the newspaper report the following week, it is noted that the lady soloist was Miss Brooks (presumably Mr Brooks' daughter) and she was accompanied by the violinist, Mr Dendy.

By the 10 March, 1877, the first edition of the 'Paignton Observer' was printed. This was to become a valuable resource in which to advertise concerts, print news and general comments about the Choral Society. It is also noted that in October, 1877, a Torquay & South Devon College of Music was founded. Under its President, Mr Charles Fowler, the Professor of Violin and Leader of the Orchestra was Mr Michael Rice and the Instructor of Choral Classes was Mr Brooks. Mr Rice was also organist at Trinity Church, Torquay, and became Conductor of the Paignton Choral Society in 1878. The College gave its first concert at the Bath Saloon, Torquay. Mr Rice was described in the local press as having "no peer as violinist in the West of England" and Mr Brooks for "many years has been identified with various musical institutions in this part of the country". He was also organist at St Andrew's Church, Paignton, which was part of the Paignton Parish Church's responsibility.

On 31 August, 1878, a brief advertisement appeared in the 'Paignton Gazette' inviting members of the Paignton Amateur Choral Society to a meeting. A booking was arranged for 4 September by George Sherriff, presumably the Secretary of the Choral Society, in a letter to the Paignton Local Health Authority requesting use of the Paignton Town Hall for that purpose. The invitation was made by Dr Pridham. It was his wife who negotiated the original hire of the Town Hall in 1871 to found the Society.

The public meeting now resolved to "resuscitate" the Society renaming it the "Paignton Choral Society" with Dr Pridham continuing as President. A subscription was fixed at a "minimum" of 5/- (25p). Dr James Alexander was appointed as Secretary and, as a close friend of Dr Pridham, within twelve months he took over the Surgery in Bishop's Place, Paignton and five years later married Dr Pridham's only daughter. Dr Alexander is mentioned frequently at this time in newspaper reports as a well-known soloist and recitalist at local social events. Mr Rice, mentioned in the previous paragraphs, became the Society's Conductor.

Rehearsals of the "brought back from the dead" Choral Society commenced on 4 October, 1878, in the Church Street Parish Schoolroom. This led to a good attendance in December for a concert in the Arena at the Singers' Oldway residence. At this stage the reader may again find a little more background of interest. Isaac Singer is described as a "self-made man", much of it through his invention of the sewing machine. When he and his wife, Isabel, moved to Torquay in 1870 because of her health, he sought, without success, a freehold site on which to build. Eventually in 1871 he acquired the Fernham Estate, twenty cottages, gardens, a large conservatory and Oldway (not the present Mansion building). On the site he constructed a large building (now known as the Rotunda) which was to be adapted either for a "theatre or circus and it was the intention to have engaged companies or artistes for the amusement of himself and friends". It later became a stabling and exercise pavilion with a wooden floor provided when entertainment functions were held. In 1873 a tender for £13,586 was accepted for the erection of a mansion (still not the present building) for Mr Singer. To return to the Society concert in the Arena, tickets were priced at 2/6d (12½ p) reserved and 1/6d (5p) for unreserved back seats. Mendelssohn's *Hear my prayer* commenced the programme followed by a number of instrument and voice solos and short choral pieces. The 'Paignton Gazette' closed its report about the concert by stating that Mr Rice made "the most in a short time of the materials at his command . . . and to the ladies and gentlemen forming the Society who all exerted themselves to the utmost. The concert was a decided success".

After a further twelve months on 22 October, 1879, the Society at the Royal Bijou Theatre performed a cantata by Cowen entitled *The Rose Maiden* together with a miscellany of other music. The choruses are reported as having been performed with precision, as were the many instrumental pieces and solos in the second half. Many requests for encores for the solo items were demanded by the audience.

It was stated earlier that 1879 would be an important date in the history of the Bijou Theatre. On 30 December the world premiere in this country, after a day postponement, was given of the operetta *The Pirates of Penzance*, or *Love of Duty* as it was also known. Whilst the copyright performance took place in Paignton by the D'Oyly Carte Company, as protection was not offered abroad for foreigners, almost simultaneously the operetta appeared on the stage in New York. The Paignton production was believed to be fairly chaotic with the costumes unready. The policemen wore sailors' garb and others in the chorus donned scarves around their heads denoting they were the pirates. The music was incomplete, and with only one rehearsal the singers had to carry their music on to the stage with them! The 'Paignton Gazette' did not pick up these problems and was more glowing in its report, describing the work "as an entirely new and original opera by WS Gilbert and Arthur Sullivan". Seating was priced at: sofa stalls – 3/- (15p); seconds – 2/- (10p); area – 1/- (5p) and gallery – 6d (2½p). It is interesting also to note that the Prime Minister, Benjamin Disraeli, was a member of the audience. Evidently he was a fairly regular visitor to Torbay and had a mistress living in Paignton. Perhaps the reports about the work at that time were being discreet with no mention of the Prime Minister's visit to the area or being at the performance? To add a few more facts about the Bijou Theatre: throughout the mid 1880's an advert frequently appeared in the local newspaper stating "The Bijou Theatre is the only room in Paignton for stage plays. DRAMATIC PERFORMANCES if given in an unlicensed Building, subjects its Proprietors and Performers to heavy penalties; and, on information being given to the Police, it will be stopped".

By the New Year, on 7 January, 1880, the Paignton Choral Society was back again at the Theatre under Mr Rice's musical direction performing a programme containing a mixture of part songs, duets, instrumental music and short choral pieces. It appears that the Conductor may have been guarded, for a reason, in restricting the choir to only short choral pieces. It is suspected they were concentrating upon the forthcoming concert in April. On the 7th of that month, at the Bijou, Mendelssohn's *Hear my prayer* was again sung with two little known cantatas today, Spohr's *God Thou art great* and Gade's *The Erle King's Daughter*. Tickets for this event were the same price as the concert two years earlier. No publicity or review of this event can be traced other than advertisements announcing the concert. This may have been because the run-up to, and results of, the General Election dominated all the columns of the local papers for some weeks. Following this concert the Society, yet again, became 'dormant'. It is noted that the census of 1861 population in Paignton was shown as 3,090. By 1881 the census recorded that this had risen to 4.461. This still small number of residents might account for the stops and starts of the Society over this period and the difficulty of finding local singers – although there is no evidence to substantiate this statement.

For music lovers, and particularly Gilbert & Sullivan 'fans', they may find an article in the 'Paignton Gazette' of interest. It is reported that the nautical operetta *HMS Pinafore* was to be performed. On the 27 and 28 July, 1880, this took place in the Pavilion on Paignton Pier which was below the low water mark making it accessible by land and water. An indication was given that for the operetta the "sisters, cousins and their aunts will come by water", and it was thought that some of the "audience would come by the same method".

As the year 1881 and 1882 progressed, it appeared that more and more theatrical and musical events were performed at the Pier Pavilion, Paignton, rather than the Bijou Theatre. The range of entertainment at the Pier was enhanced by the installation of a large two-manual organ and a moveable stage.

On 23 November, 1882, the Foundation Stone was laid for another establishment, the Temperance Hall in New Street, Paignton which would be used by the Good Templars. It was built at a cost of £400 and was eventually opened for a meeting of the congregation on Whit Monday, 21 May, the following year. The Upper Hall was used by the Good Templars and the ground floor as a storeroom. The Kelly's publication in 1883 stated that the Hall was not to be let for entertainments but this rule appears to have changed subsequently. Various social and cultural events, including concerts by the Paignton Choral Society, took place in the Hall which had a capacity to accommodate up to "four hundred persons".

By January, 1883, a Musical Society was inaugurated with meetings in the Pier Pavilion to which "vocalists and instrumentalists" were invited to attend. It does not appear that this was anything to do with the Paignton Choral Society and was probably a way of promoting the Pier's frequent musical events.

On 26 October, 1884, Mr Arthur Waycott, who had been organist at the Parish Church for the past seven years, played his last service. His successor, Mr Frank Harris from Oxford, was appointed as the new organist from a list of thirty applicants. His name will appear frequently in the coming pages as Conductor of the Choral Society and many other music organisations.

There is little need to record the popularity of some of the more traditional oratorios, such as the *Messiah*, and to this work should be added Mendelssohn's *Elijah*. In April, 1885, Torquay Musical Society, a new society established in Autumn 1884 under the conductorship of Mr Rice, achieved a "great triumph" with a performance of the latter work in the Bath Saloon, Torquay - a building standing roughly on the site of the 'Living Coasts' tourist attraction. It is reported that the Hall was packed to capacity – at least one thousand people with the performers. It was further stated in the 'Torquay Directory & South Devon Journal' that "hundreds of people gathered around the north door to gain an entry; by some of these the door was forced, the policeman in charge rolled over, and in came the crowd of persons into a part of the saloon which was already over-crowded . . . the gangways and every available space was occupied with people who were content with standing room". Even "forms from a young ladies' seminary, half-a-mile distant" were carried to the Hall and still hundreds of people were turned away. What some choirs would do to have that attendance! By December this successful Society had a membership of fifty two vocalists and one hundred and sixty honorary members.

It is interesting to note that in January after the concert , the Honorary Secretary of the Torquay Musical Society wrote a lengthy letter to the 'Torquay Directory & South Devon Journal' entitled "Concert Expenses". He expressed an opinion that many members of an audience experiencing a full house had no idea of the margin between receipts and expenditure. He continued by stating that "no oratorio could be performed here under ninety pounds" and to spend less could result in "an indifferent perform-ance". It was essential that each concert should pay for itself and he quoted the figures for the excellent *Elijah* concert held by the Society the previous April. Receipts and expenditure had been just under £100 each leaving a profit of only £3.6.10 (£3.34). That sounds familiar using equivalent figures today.

To now pick up the threads of the Paignton Musical Society, at the General Meeting on 26 October, 1885, not to be confused with the two societies just mentioned earlier, Mr Harris and Mr Samuel Martin were appointed as Joint Conductors. Mr Harris, as already mentioned, was Organist and Choirmaster at the Parish Church and Mr Martin held a similar post at Christ Church, Paignton, as well as having a musical business in Paignton and he was also a private tutor. The Secretary to the Society was Rev James Hamlyn, Headmaster of the Paignton Preparatory School ("a school for gentlemen's sons") and a competent violinist. If you are confused by the name "Musical Society", it is certain that this was the former Paignton Choral Society re-activated. At this meeting a programme was suggested, but by the time of the concert in the Temperance Hall on 27 January, 1886, this had totally changed. The "chorus of eighty perform-ers" was conducted by Mr Harris with Mr Martin as accompanist. Another rather unheard-of cantata in this day and age, Anderton's *Wreck of the Hesperus* was performed. The subsequent report in the 'Devon County Standard' stated that the singers numbered about sixty and the performance was "musically of a high character". During the year it is noted that Mr

16

Harris was busy in other fields as Conductor of the Paignton Orchestral Society as well as undertaking his duties as Organist in the Parish Church and private tutoring of piano, violin, organ, singing and voice culture.

On 19 May, 1886, the Temperance Hall was again used by the now-known Paignton Musical Society for its second concert of the season. A "crowded and appreciative audience" listened to the first half of miscellaneous melodies and Romberg's *The Lay of the Bell* after the interval. A "corps musicale" of about a hundred vocal and instrumental performers appeared in the concert. Dr Alexander sang in a quartet and septet with the Rev Hamlyn, again a soloist in the programme.

Mr Dendy's remarkable and valuable contribution to Paignton's development has already been mentioned and his death on 13 August, 1886, after a short illness, was a tragic blow for the town. It will be remembered that he financed the building of the Gerston Hotel, the first hotel in Paignton with the adjoining Bijou Theatre. He was described as the man who converted the town from a "mere fishing village to a rising and fashionable watering place and health resort". It is worth recording a number of his achievements which Mr Dendy created for the benefit of Paignton residents and its visitors. In addition to the Gerston Hotel, he financed the conversion of two villas, with a tower attached, which were then connected to become the Esplanade Hotel (now the 'Inn on the Green'). He purchased the Teignmouth Pier for £1,100 believing it to be the very thing for Paignton. However, the cost of removing the piles was more than the value of the Pier, so he decided to build a new structure from scratch on the Paignton sea-front. In 1871 he started a bathing accommodation company with "fifty well-appointed bathing machines" on the sands. He also established a printing firm to print his own bills and it later produced the 'Paignton Observer & Echo' and the 'Devon County Standard'. Many extracts from both newspapers have been used to compile this history. He started the first horse-bus company which it was thought would never pay against quicker and cheaper rail travel, but it did pay by delivering its passengers direct into the centre of Torquay and Paignton towns. By sea, he established a "steam launch" service plying between Torquay harbour and the Paignton promenade with boats every half hour. He was also a many-sided man and amongst his social activities he was a very accomplished violinist. It is said he could often be found in the Pier Pavilion with his Stradivarius violin and an accompanist playing classical music.

To refer back to the Bijou Theatre, in April, 1887, the scenery, wardrobe, seating and effects (including fifty oil paintings) were put up for sale. Six months later Mr Dendy's wife, Eliza, died. In October, 1887, the Dendy's residence was sold, and Mr Denby's 1718 Stradivarius violin went at auction for £375. With his other violins a total of £2,500 was raised in that day. To complete the record: at 11.00pm on 15 March, 1986, "Time, gentlemen please" was called when the Gerston Hotel closed for the last time. The New Bijou Theatre, as it seems it was now called, had been given notice in September 1985 to quit performances. When demolition eventually took place of the Hotel, the Theatre mahogany and gilt proscenium was installed in the Public Hall and other property in the Pier Pavilion, Paignton. The memory of Mr Dendy lives today. The main arterial road into the centre of town is Hyde Road, using Mr Dendy's second Christian name, and a side road off Hyde Road and opposite the site of the former Bijou Theatre is named Dendy Road.

Back to the 27 September, 1886, at the Parish Church Schoolroom, Church Street, Paignton: the AGM appointed a Committee and Officers with the Rev Hamlyn continuing as Secretary. The following week the 'Paignton Gazette' and 'Devon County Standard' both reported on the meeting of the new 'Paignton Choral Society'. For the next two years there appears to have been confusion in reporting about the Society, described in some places as the 'Paignton Choral Society' and others as the 'Paignton Musical Society'. A performance of the *May Queen* was planned to be performed just before Christmas under the Society Conductor, Mr Harris. An offer was made by the local supplier, Paish's Music Shop in Dartmouth Place, Paignton (and Fleet Street, Torquay) that the music could be purchased at a discount price of 2d (about 1p) off the cost of the score – 1/- (5p). It was on Thursday, 20 January, 1887, that the *May Queen* performance eventually took place in the Temperance Hall with a "band and chorus of one hundred and twenty performers ... and all went well from the first to the last note". The January event was followed by a concert on 1 June, Whit Monday, with Handel's oratorio *Judas Maccabaeus* in the same Hall. Amongst the principal soloists the Rev Hamyln's name appears. Some performers received requests for encores, but the audience attendance "was not such as the excellence of the performance warranted". It is suspected that local citizens, like most others in the country, were heavily engaged in the preparations for the 20 June celebrating Queens Victoria's Gold Anniversary of her accession to the throne.

Looking further into the subject of entertainment, two events appeared in the local newspapers which seem relevant to the arts. In July, 1887, the owners of the Paignton Pier Pavilion applied to the Torquay Magistrates for a theatrical licence. It was refused on the grounds that it was not a suitable place for the purpose but despite no objections from rival houses the magistrates stuck to their guns. Two months later in September, 1887, a major tragedy occurred for the entertainment industry when an Exeter Theatre burnt down with the loss of almost two hundred people, from an audience estimated at between seven and eight hundred. It appears that one of the act-drops in a play suddenly descended, hitting the stage gaslight jets causing a rapid and horrendous fire. The subsequent inquest found that the building had been badly designed with poor attention paid to fire-proofing and many inadequate and narrow passages included. At one stage the architect and lessee of the Theatre faced criminal charges, but these were subsequently dropped as it was felt many parties were to blame for the resulting loss of life. In the aftermath of this tragedy, the Paignton Local Board reviewed all the public places in Paignton, including the Temperance Hall and local churches, to examine the means of exit in case of a fire or panic. It recommended immediate action to ensure external doors were changed so that they opened outwards.

A month later, in October, 1887, it was reported that the new season of the Paignton Choral Society would commence with a large number of members joining and a successful season predicted with the planned work, *St Cecilia*. This optimism was short-lived, when six months later it was announced that practices had been discontinued because of an "inadequate amount of public support".

It is noted over the next few years, right up to the turn of the century, advertisements in the local papers inserted by Mr Harris for private tuition stated he was the "Conductor of the Paignton Orchestral Society founded in 1887". It is assumed that members of the "Band" reported to have played in the performance of the M*ay Queen* by the Choral Society, were possibly the 'fledglings' of this new group.

On 26 April, 1887, a second Church of England building in Paignton, Christ Church, had its Foundation Stone laid. Compared to the Parish Church, this new lofty early English Gothic-style structure without a chancel screen and far greater seating capacity for six hundred congregation and an extra one hundred easily accommodated on chairs, was planned to have had a spire built at the south-west end. At a cost of £5,676, excluding the adjoining iron hut and boundary wall, funds did not permit the building of the spire and, in fact, this never materialized. The building was consecrated by the Bishop of Exeter on 1 June, 1888. It is interesting to note that, when it first opened, it was surrounded by fields and that the Vicar complained that noise of the tractors working in the area interrupted his Sunday sermons. Much later, with the increasing use of automobiles, horns sounding at the cross roads at the west end of the Church were causing similar problems in Church services. Eventual widening of the main road was welcomed by clergy and congregation. The excellent acoustics in the Church made it a useful venue for concerts by the Society from the mid-twentieth century and again into the twenty-first century.

On Tuesday, 23 October, 1888, the General Meeting of the Paignton Musical Society was again held in the Church Street Schoolroom. Attendance was so small that it was agreed the Society should remain in abeyance until former members decided that they "wished to commence active work". If sufficient new members came forward, a further meeting would be called. With no funds in hand the Secretary, Rev Hamlyn, was prevented from mailing out to members or intended members. In fact the support to restart the Society does not appear to have been forthcoming for another seven years.

It is of value to report here that a 'rival', the Torquay Musical Society mentioned earlier and referring to the performance of *Elijah* under Mr Rice as its Conductor who also conducted the Paignton Choral Society in 1878 and 1879, had enjoyed three successful years of concerts. However, in January, 1889, this Society also had to cease because of "all interest in it having died out" and its numbers had dropped from one hundred and sixty-three to thirty-two. Not to be thwarted, one month later Mr Rice had established a Choral Society at St Marychurch, Torquay, and by March it was reported that it "numbered over one hundred".

The national census two years later showed that the population of Paignton had now reached 6,783. This rise in ten years of 2,322 was reported as the greatest proportional increase in any town in the country. If the St Marychurch Choral Society could suddenly find singers, why was the Choral Society in Paignton unable to do so with this population rise? Mr Rice was also conducting the Torquay Orchestral Society. Sadly the St Marychurch Society suffered a set-back on the 13 February, 1890 when he died and a concert was given in St Marychurch Town Hall the following month in his memory.

Music appeared to be alive elsewhere as it was reported that the famous musician Sir Charles Hallé, knighted in 1888 and previously mentioned at the start of this chapter, with Lady Hallé, a brilliant violinist, gave a performance at the Bath Saloon, Torquay, prior to their two year tour of Australia.

To digress again, in writing about places of entertainment: twenty years after the building of the Gerston Hotel with its Bijou Theatre, the foundations of the Public Hall in Palace Avenue were laid in January, 1890. As far back as October, 1886, offers of contributions into a Guarantee Fund for the Hall had been organised by Mr George Campbell who had been appointed honorary secretary of the Fund. At that time it was stated that an "eligible site had been selected in a central position adjacent to the Dartmouth Road". A guarantee of £150 per annum for five years was required in order that the work could commence. The Public Hall was designed by George Bridgman, a local architect who planned Paignton Hospital and dozens of buildings and structures all over South Devon; the 'Wigwam' at Oldway, and the United Reformed Church referred to earlier in this history. The Public Hall consisted of a drill hall with an armoury and committee room on the ground floor and, above, a large hall with a platform and two dressing rooms behind the stage, cloakrooms and an adjoining caretaker's apartment. The main hall was capable of seating eight hundred people, which could be increased by a further two hundred "if closely packed" and even twelve to fourteen hundred if the seating was removed. It was also possible to partition-off the area under the gallery to create a smaller room for meetings or an anteroom for functions in the main hall. The Public Hall built by Mr GF Yeo cost £2,435, with some of this expense being met through shares sold by the Public Hall Company, with Dr Alexander as Chairman since August, 1891. The official opening of the Hall in September, 1890, included in the concert the Paignton Orchestral Society conducted by Mr Harris. The playing of a violincello obligato by Franklin Singer is reported as having taken the audience "by storm". Decoration of the Hall for its opening with plants, ferns and flowers was provided by another well-known Paignton family, a Mr William Rossiter, a local nurseryman in Fernham House, Torquay Road, Paignton (telephone number 534!). It was lit by gas when it first opened and within a month the Company members were most anxious to install electricity into the Public Hall. It appears that by November, 1889, a charity entertainment stated that electric light would be used in the Hall for the first time. Following its official opening, the Hall was in high demand with bookings nearly every night including church groups, lectures, music and meetings of the Paignton Athenaeum Society. For a while there was a problem in the presentation of dramatic performances because Devon County Council refused to grant a licence owing to inadequate exit points. Health and safety reared its head even then, although the experience of the fire and resulting deaths in the Exeter Theatre mentioned earlier probably made officials very cautious before licences were granted. The Public Hall Company also purchased the Temperance Hall for £380 which had been used for many social and cultural events including the Paignton Choral Society. It was re-let to organisations for 10/- (50p) per night. The reason for devoting this amount of space to the Public Hall is justified, because the Choral Society would be using it on numerous occasions as the history will show. The Hall was later known as the Palace Avenue Theatre and would go through various stages of development and refurbishment in the next two centuries.

At this stage we turn our attention to another section of the local music world and what became the Paignton Operatic Society. Two local prominent business men, Mr Robert Waycott and Mr Harry Rossiter, were prime movers in creating the Society. What had started off at rehearsals as a choral work was changed as the members generated enthusiasm to turn *HMS Pinafore* into a full-blown opera presentation. Thus, on Thursday and Friday 29 and 30 January, 1891, in the Public Hall, the Operatic Society with a chorus of forty voices gave "an ambitious performance" of the Gilbert & Sullivan work with proceeds donated to the Cottage Hospital. The Society claimed it was the first amateur company in England to present *HMS Pinafore* although this was challenged by a society in the North! Mr Harris conducted and also played the organ, with Mr Martin as pianist and the Royal Prussian Band filling in the orchestral section in the programme. Some thirty-five years later, Mr Rossiter, one of the founder members of the Operatic Society, observed that at the performances a local Brixham man, Mr Robert Cayme, who took the important role of Sir Joseph Porter "could not sing the part as his own voice was not good enough". A member of the chorus sang the songs whilst Mr Cayme mimed his part, although he was stated to be "a very fine actor". The production was a very amateurish event with no professional coach and scenery painted and dresses made by members of the Society. Despite all of this, the newspapers of the time reported that the Society had "diligently been practising for months". The Operatic Society was under the patronage of members of the Singer family and Dr Alexander. The association, with the involvement of the Choral Society's Conductors (Messrs Harris and Martin), would appear to indicate that members of that Society may well have participated in the performances.

In September, 1891, the Rev Frederick Poland, Vicar of the Parish Church, wrote a farewell note to his congregation in the Parish Magazine. He was originally inducted at the Church in June, 1861. Earlier in the year his thirty-year old daughter had died and it is assumed that this, and other pressures in his duties, may have hastened his decision to leave. The following January, the Rev Dr John Trelawny-Ross, curate at St Andrew's Church, Bournemouth, accepted the living. He was formally inducted to the post on 21 April, 1892, by the Archdeacon of Totnes and later became a President of the Choral Society.

We need to step back for the moment to 1879 when Mr Dendy financed the building of the Pier and its Pavilion in Paignton. Its construction created controversy for which Mr Dendy was not unknown because it was seen to be encroaching on to Polsham Green as it was then known. Over the following years the Pier was to be sold to various business syndicates, and individuals, with the Council also having the opportunity to purchase it. However, the latter was not taken up because of eventual contract problems. The Pier Pavilion hosted regular concerts, often using its fine two manual organ, as well as other theatrical events. Twenty-eight years later, as will be recorded in Chapter 2, tragedy was to hit the Pier, now owned by the Devon Dock, Pier and Steamship Company, when the pier-head was totally destroyed by fire.

The year of 1893 saw a number of musical activities being held despite the non-appearance of the Choral Society. On Monday, 28 March, at the invitation of the Paignton Athenaeum, Mr Martin conducted a selection of pieces from *Messiah*. It is reported that a "local choir of about fifty voices had been carefully selected and trained" by him. Seventeen days later on 6 April, a "Dramatic and Musical Entertainment" was held in the Public Hall for the "benefit of Mr Harris". On the 24th of that month Mr Harris was busy with a "Closing Entertainment" by the Brixham Choral Union and the Paignton Orchestral Society. As a concert item, Bennett's *May Queen* again made its appearance with a band and chorus of "eighty performers". During this year another gentleman, Mr Alfred Macey, Professor of Music, Organist and Choirmaster at St Barnabus Church, Torquay, and pianoforte tutor at HMS Britannia (which was then a Naval training ship anchored on the Dart at Dartmouth before the College was built), advertised his singing classes at a private address in Palace Avenue, Paignton. On the 26 October, a further advertisement appeared under his name for the "Paignton Musical Society 1893-4" inviting members to attend a "first choral practice" at the end of the month. The first rehearsal night would decide which cantata would be prepared. The subscription was fixed at 5/- (25p) and honorary members 10/6d (52½p). Once again, were some members of the dormant Paignton Choral Society amongst any of these singing groups? It is strongly suspected they were!

In researching the history of the Society, the author of this book, as an aside, felt that any music-loving reader would find the following report amusing. In October, 1889, a dedication took place of the Paignton Parish organ which had cost over £2000 and had been donated as a gift by Paris Singer. In August, 1893, the Vicar, Rev Dr Trelawny-Ross, commented in his Parish Magazine on the Choir Festival in the Church. The following is a quote from that publication – "Mr Harris accompanied the service with effect; a difficult task at all times, owing to the distances between the Choir and organist; a still more difficult task with the swell organ useless". Just over twelve months later, on 1 November, 1894, a Vestry Meeting in the Town Hall was held to discuss the proposed "removal of the organ in the Parish Church to the south of the choir, the position occupied by the former organ". The instrument at the time was situated in the Tower at a distance of 90ft (nearly 27½m) from the Choir and between them was the congregation. The 'Paignton Observer' in a lengthy report of the meeting stated "At times the singers could not hear the organ, and could not distinguish what melody was being played. He (the Vicar) had tried himself at times to find out what was going on at the organ and had to give up . . . Then look at it from the organist's (Mr Harris) point of view. He could not hear the choir, and often had to violate the principles of organ playing and raise his hands to try and find out where they were, and playing in a chopping way, as distressing to him as to all musical people. And then, with regard to the congregation. He would omit the noises caused by the gas engine, which were a terror to nervous visitors (hear, hear) by the preparation of the organ for playing . . . Mr A, who was close to the organ, was grumbling at the choir, which he considered was always behind, while Mr B, who was near the choir, was grumbling at the organ as always behind the choir". It was considered that "here was a good instrument placed in a bad position and subject to dust, to extremes of draughts and variations of temperature" all of which had done considerable harm to the organ. The blowing of the organ by hand and a water instead of a gas engine were all discussed at the Vestry meeting but re-siting of the instrument was prevented because of the question of funds. Within a short while of this meeting, organ fund-raising activities were taking place. A concert twelve months later by Mr Harris, with the Paignton Parish Choir and Paignton Orchestral Society, was held and included music from Purcell's *Macbeth* as a major item in the general programme. It is quite possible, amidst all this turmoil over the position of the organ, that some members of the Choral Society were also members of the Parish Church Choir. The organ finally broke down in April, 1906, and had to be rebuilt after which it came into service again the following October in its new position at the east end of the Church.

It was at a meeting in the Ballroom of the emporium at Bailey's Assembly Rooms, Victoria Street, Paignton, in September, 1895, that a further attempt was made for the "resuscitation" of the Society. Dr Alexander, mentioned earlier, chaired the meeting attended by "other gentlemen experienced in the working of Musical Societies"! The Chairman is reported as having said that the old Society had split because of too many ornamental members – "passengers in the boat" – and he urged that those joining should "be really singing members". On the matter of subscriptions, it was emphasized that this should not be out of the reach of working men. A 5/- (25p) subscription was agreed, although a suggestion that male choristers from a church choir should be admitted on special terms was put forward, but not agreed. Mr Harris offered to conduct the Society and the meeting adjourned so that the town and neighbourhood could be canvassed for potential members. The following Monday, about fifty ladies and gentlemen had indicated that they wished to join. A Committee was formed with the Rev Hugh Pinchin, a Curate at the Parish Church since July 1891, as Secretary and Treasurer. Handel's *Messiah* was a possible work to be rehearsed, but by early October this had changed to Mendelssohn's *Hymn of Praise*. At the first session in Bailey's Emporium, attendance was not the success it was thought it might have been as some people did not know about the rehearsal. A viewpoint in the 'Devon County Standard' advised that the new society should guard against "cliqueism – the downfall of most successful choral societies"!

Whilst the Society was now rehearsing the *Hymn of Praise*, a little space is robbed from this history to add another aside. On 5 March, 1896, a column 'Local Lucubrations' appeared in the 'Paignton Observer and Echo' written by "A Flaneur". To quote the remark in full: "A considerable time has elapsed Mr Editor, since I last contributed a few stray jottings. As you were so frequently suffering from want of space and I was continually 'crowded out' the notes discontinued; but as I understand you are about to enlarge the space available for local news, I will with your permission – whenever there is anything to chat about, and always providing the spirit moves – inflict a few jottings from time to time". For those who are unaware, the word "flaneur" is French for an "idler or loafer" and "lucubration" is Latin for a "treatise or literary work of a pedantic or elaborate character"! "Flaneur" will be mentioned frequently as an important agitator in encouraging the Society to restart after a number of lapses in its existence. The column was later renamed "Here and There" and "Flaneur" may well have been written by another person who obviously still had sympathetic musical interests.

Six months later, in April, 1896, the *Hymn of Praise* was performed in the Public Hall with tickets priced at 2/- (10p) for front seats, 1/- (5p) second seats and the front two rows of the gallery 1/6d (7½p). The two and a half hour programme included "madrigals, glees and instrumental music" and the Hall is reported to have been "well filled in every part". The reporter reviewing the concert commented that the "bass was too few in numbers and the tenor hardly sufficient to balance the soprano and alto" singers, but despite this they were praised for their timing and precision. How many times will the reader see this comment made about the male section of the Choral Society in the coming pages?

In October the members were called to a meeting in the Lower Room in the Public Hall with Mr William Goodale, Churchwarden of the Parish Church, presiding. The accounts of the Society showed 15/- (75p) deficit. The Secretary, Rev Pinchin, announced his resignation, not, it is hastened to add, because of the financial situation but because he was leaving the Parish soon for a new appointment in Wandsworth. A further problem was raised at the Meeting because the rehearsal room at Bailey's Emporium had now become a showroom, so a new venue had to be found for practices. Mr Frank Palk, a local hosier, hatter and glover and shirt maker in Palace Avenue became Secretary, and rehearsals returned to an 'old haunt' mentioned earlier in this book, the Gerston Hotel Assembly Rooms. Iliffe's cantata *Morning* and Barnett's *Ancient Mariner* were selected as works for the next concert. Subscriptions remained at 5/- (25p) for the session or half this amount for a half-session. A note in the 'Paignton Observer and Echo' appeared two weeks after the rehearsals had started stating the Brixham

Choral Society would be joining the Paignton Society for the concert. A further report just before Christmas 1896, promised that Mr Harris' Orchestral Society would participate and be "one of the best ever heard in Paignton". It appears pressure was being put on all the Society singers at this stage of rehearsals as a newspaper advertisement stated that there would be no "Christmas recess!"

It may be interesting to note that in December, 1896, a Juvenile Operetta of "Snow White and the Seven Dwarfs" was performed for the NSPCC by young members of the Band of Mercy and children belonging to the League of Pity. It appears that this group was, or developed into, the Juvenile Operetta Company under the direction of Mr Harris.

When the Paignton Choral Society concert eventually took place in the Public Hall on 11 January, 1897, the *Ancient Mariner* had been dropped for a performance later in the year. Glees, ballads and quartets with a Mozart symphony replaced the work. The orchestra of nearly thirty players appears to have lived up to its pre-publicity and it was reported that a "finer band of instrumentalists has never been heard here". Although the Barnett work was not included in the programme, the chorus still performed Dr Fredrick Iliffe's pastoral cantata *Morning*, composed originally for the Cheltenham Triennial Festival, with the choir now reported in the local paper as small, but effective, and that good training was stated to be amply evidenced. "A large and fashionable" audience attended, according to the 'Paignton Observer and Echo' with the 'Devon County Standard' describing them as "the elite of the district", but the "pecuniary results" were unsatisfactory. The report on the Thursday following the concert ended by stating that the choral practice of the *Ancient Mariner* would commence the following Monday. Although no further reports of the Society are recorded until October, the Brixham Musical Society (it is assumed this was the Brixham Choral Society referred to in the previous page and which joined the Paignton Choral Society for their January performance) presented the *Ancient Mariner* in April. The concert in the Brixham Market Hall (not the Scala Theatre as we know it but the main building housing a youth project and Council offices) was conducted by Mr Harris and accompanied by the Paignton Orchestral Society.

In Autumn an advertisement stated that practices for the Paignton Choral Society would start in the Gerston Hall after the Summer break. However, two weeks later these had moved to Mr Harris' house in Sefton Terrace, Dartmouth Road, Paignton. In view of the financial problems of the Society, could they not afford to pay for the hire of the Gerston Rooms? Shortly after the date mentioned, the *Ancient Mariner* appears to have sailed into oblivion as did the Society for the next eight years. On the 17 February the following year, 1898, 'Turned Up' was advertised as a three act farcical comedy performed by members of the Paignton Operatic and Dramatic

Society assisted by officers from HMS Britannia. Five days later, in the Public Hall under the direction of Mr Harris, the event took place which, it was stated, would be in aid of the funds for the Operatic group and to clear the debt of the Paignton Choral Society.

The collapse, yet again, of the Choral Society was not echoed by the Operatic Society, which had successfully performed *HMS Pinafore* in 1891, and after a six year gap now presented three Gilbert & Sullivan operettas each performed in the Public Hall over a period of two years. In May, 1897, *Pirates of Penzance* took the stage with an augmented band from the Torquay Theatre. *Gondoliers* followed in April, 1898, and *HMS Pinafore* again in December. However, the Public Hall performances were never filled and the operettas were produced at a loss. Locally, over the next three years three Conductors, Mr Harris, Mr Macey mentioned in earlier pages, and Mr Martin who was joint Conductor of the Choral Society in 1886 and currently organist/choirmaster at Christ Church, were actively involved in local music. An interesting comment was made in the local press when, concerning the performance of Mendelssohn's *St Paul* (Part II) with Mr Martin's Choral Class in December, 1897, at his Church, it was stated that a "large congregation number, we should say somewhere about nine hundred attended". Earlier in this chapter it was noted that the seating in the Church for the congregation was about seven hundred to be accommodated on seats. Was the nine hundred audience for the concert newspaper licence in reporting, or did some members stand throughout the performance which happened at times for events in the Public Hall? In July, 1898, bearing in mind how fickle the British weather is, Mr Martin's group took a gamble and gave an open-air concert in the grounds of the Esplanade Hotel with the cantata the *Sherwood Queen* selected. Mr Harris also appears to have been busy with his Orchestral Society when, for his "benefit", a concert was given in January, 1898, also in the Public Hall. The event was joined by the Junior Operetta group performing the *Enchanted Rose*.

As the turn of the century approached, the music scene continued without a Choral Society in Paignton. Mr Harris still appears to have found plenty to occupy his time as Organist and Choirmaster at Paignton Parish Church, as an accompanist at music events and with his Orchestral Society performing at garden parties, fetes and concerts. Mrs Alexander (you may remember her husband was Chairman of the Choral Society from September, 1895 to October, 1896) also made regular appearances as soloist and as a leading actress in musicals. Against this, the Operatic Society was suddenly in jeopardy when its highly competent Stage Manager left the area.

Just before the end of the twentieth century, at an Extra-ordinary Meeting of the Public Hall shareholders, permission was given to borrow a sum not exceeding £1,000 to provide a scenery dock, improvements to the kitchen accommodation and an additional room for public meetings. The latter was anticipated to cost £650 from the sum borrowed. The staging area had already been improved with an extra wing and a couple more dressing rooms added backstage. In October, 1899, the Paignton Orchestral Society held its first Promenade Concert in the Public Hall as an experiment. The 'Paignton Observer and Echo' carried an advertisement describing the event as "Immense Attraction; Professional Vocalists; Music Up-to-Date; Elegant Decorations; Bright Pleasing music, Light Refreshments all at 1/- (5p) and 6d (2½p) admission price". The newspaper further reported that "those possessing chair tickets can procure checks which will enable them to promenade and resume their seats when they so desire". The article went on to say that "the event was not patronized as it should have been, the proceeds being hardly satisfactory". Mr Harris, however, persevered with two further Promenade concerts over the following consecutive months.

One year into the new century, on 22 January, 1901, one event dominated the news. The death of Queen Victoria, after sixty-four years of an outstanding reign, shook the nation which subsequently paid homage to her at the very large State Funeral.

To return to music: in May, 1901, the Paignton Operatic Society, after agitation by the local press and reference to the successful societies in Torquay and Teignmouth, performed *Les Cloches de Corneville*. However, it is noted that the last act had to be abruptly drawn to a conclusion in the middle of it, because officers, cadets and others on HMS Britannia had to catch the last train to Kingswear! It was claimed that this rather spoilt the plot in the opera. Following this performance 'Flaneur' took the opportunity to have a 'dig' at his neighbouring towns and it was felt that his comments may bring a smile to the face of the reader of this history. "Now that the Paignton Operatic Society has brought its rehearsals and performances to a close, congratulations of the Paignton public may fairly be expressed through the medium of the Press to all who worked so harmoniously and well towards the splendid success achieved. With the exception of a few biased persons whose obvious motive is envy (and who do not reside here, but in an adjacent town where a similar society exists) high praise is accorded to the efforts of the Paignton amateurs, the feeling of visitors and strangers being one of intense amazement that little Paignton can produce such an opera in so splendid a style".

The following year the Operatic Society performed again under Mr Harris' conductorship. It appears that his talents also extended to his son who won a Scholarship to study at the Exeter Cathedral School from September, 1903. On 8 December in that year the death of Rev Poland, Vicar of the Parish Church from 1861 to 1891, was recorded. Just over twelve months later in January, 1905, the sad loss of Dr Alexander, aged fifty seven, and referred to many times from 1878 to the end of that century in the previous pages of this book, occurred. His funeral was an enormous local event with two hundred wreaths accompanying the coffin, and about two thousand people attending his funeral or lining the cortege route.

A letter in the 'Paignton Observer and Echo' on 5 January, 1905, may again be found amusing with its now rather out-dated phraseology, " Dear Sir, I am advised by several persons of taste and influence that a good opportunity occurs for the revival of oratorio in Paignton. I agree . . . Let me add that all who can sing should join; for in a Choral Society there are no reasons, as there may possibly be in others, for restricting membership to one or two social groups. It must be a town affair and all sections welcomed, Faithfully yours, Frank Harris ". This letter appears to have had the desired effect when a meeting the following week was held to form a Philharmonic Society including choral and orchestral classes. Mr Harris and Mr Frank Benson, Organist and Choirmaster at Christ Church, Paignton, were appointed as Joint Conductors. As it was to be a short season, a subscription was confirmed at 2/- (10p) with each succeeding member of a family paying 1/6d (7½p) with the loan of music included. The Executive Committee agreed that Mendelssohn's *Athalie*, together with an orchestral work and motet, would be performed and that practices would start on 24 January in the Lower Schoolroom, Church Street, Paignton. Anyone with "a voice of even moderate power will be welcomed" was the encouragement from the members at the meeting. This publicity to start a Choral Group appears to have worked as, when the concert was held on 11 April, a "band and chorus of one hundred" (seventy vocalists and twenty seven orchestra) performed. An extract from *The Creation – The Heavens are telling* concluded the concert. The 'Paignton Observer and Echo' report stressed, yet again, "the paucity of males in the chorus, this somewhat weakening the balance of voices" of the Choral Society.

One wonders whether there was such a thing as inflation in those days? Twenty eight years ago it was recorded that seat prices were 2/6d (12½p) and 1/- (5p) with the gallery in the Public Hall 1/6d (7½ p). The prices for this April concert were identical. Following the performance of *Athalie*, our friend and agitator Flaneur, in welcoming the concert given by the Philharmonic Society, felt that it might tackle a big work. *Elijah*, *St Paul* or *Messiah* were suggested. Again this hint and publicity seem to have succeeded, with rehearsals in Christ Church Schoolroom, Paignton, starting the following October for *Elijah*. One month later, using the pseudonym " Korahite", a letter far too long to produce here appeared in the 'Paignton Observer and Echo'. It appears that by then Korahite, who was probably a member of the Paignton Philharmonic Society Committee, indicated that it had been decided to postpone *Elijah* rehearsals as "so great a work demands much time, very sedulous practice and devotion and co-operation on the part of a large number of persons". In stressing the need for singers, he (it is assumed it was a gentleman) observed how successful music was in other parts of the country. "In the Northern counties of England, artisans, tired after a day's work, will walk or cycle miles to an evening practice". He went on to write "Cannot we have something like this in Paignton? Surely if anything is worth enthusiasm besides "Rugger" it is really good music! If the members of the church choirs, boys and all, would come, the thing would be done and others would follow". His parting shot in the letter: "Besides, why should people go to Torquay for music?"

In November the local music scene suffered a further blow in that the Paignton Operatic Society had ceased to exist, although similar societies in Torquay and Teignmouth appeared to be quite active. A further blow occurred when at a special Committee meeting on Monday 22 January, 1906, it was resolved that the practices for the Philharmonic Society "be discontinued until the autumn". In fact, again, these were delayed and did not start until January, 1907. Flaneur suggested that in a town of ten thousand inhabitants there was a need for both amateur operatic and choral societies.

At Christmas Day service, 1907, the Rev Dr Trelawny-Ross, Vicar for sixteen years at the Parish Church and President of the Choral Society for most of that time, preached his last sermon. He resigned because of bad health.

The following Summer, further hard-hitting words were uttered, this time by Dr Cummings of the Guildhall School of Music in an address at Southport. He expressed an opinion that "Devonians are not a musical people, the Devonshire climate being too soft and enervating, people there take things too easily and not troubling about the morrow". To rub it in more deeply, he added that "the most moderate singing in the North was better than the best in the South". Fighting talk to the 'Paignton Observer' columnist, who again pushed for the revival of the Choral Society, the demise of which he blamed on the "sheer inertia on the part of the male voice portion"! The Operatic Society had also remained in abeyance from 1905 until April, 1907, although music did not entirely die in Paignton with the Paignton Orchestral Society, church choirs and visiting professional music groups all active.

It was not until November, 1909, with apparently no pre-press publicity, that the Choral Society suddenly announced that it had reverted to its old name and would be holding a concert in December. Under a newly appointed conductor, Mr Wilfred Layton, organist at the Britannia Royal Naval College, Part II of Mendelssohn's *Hymn of Praise* was the main work with a "band and chorus of about one hundred". Building on the success of this concert, the following March a selection from Part II of Haydn's *Creation*, Beethoven's *Choral Fantasia* and Elgar's *The Snow* were performed in the Public Hall. One of the soloists was Mr Alfred Layton, father of the conductor. In September two successive weeks of advertisement appeared inviting members of the Society to attend practices in the Parish Church Schoolrooms for the next concert to be held on the "34th" of December! Brahms' *Song of Destiny* and Mendelssohn's *Lorely* were to be featured. The concert, in fact on 14 December, seemed again to have been a part family affair with Miss Margaret Layton, the conductor's daughter who had become a professional singer, as soprano soloist.

For 1911, with Easter approaching, a traditional work for that time of the year was included in the March concert in the Public Hall. A selection from *Messiah* was offered plus Gounod's motet *Gallia* with two soloists from Exeter Cathedral appearing in the concert. By this time the Society was said to be on a sound footing financially. It also appears at this stage that the author of 'Local Lucubrations' had very much taken to heart the comments made by the lecturer from the Guildhall School of Music in 1908. He believed that Devon was suffering from "indifference" and not a "lack of musical qualities". He was delighted that a permanent town musical society had been established, but hitherto "want of interest on the part of male singers had killed such efforts". The columnist continued by writing that he hoped that the Society would be a "thoroughly town one for all sections and classes of the community and with an open seasame to all vocalists to come and join". He referred back to a word used in a report some time back, 'cliqueism', and hoped that the Society "will be no sectional affair" and "that an open encouragement will be given to all sundry who are sufficiently interested and able to sing to join". A sign of class divisions at that time?

With the country rejoicing, following the Coronation of King George V with his wife Queen Mary in June, rehearsals commenced in September in St Andrew's Schoolrooms, Paignton, for a December performance of Coleridge-Taylor's *Song of Hiawatha* which included the *Wedding Feast* and the *Death of Minnehaha*. The work would be featured many times in future concerts of the Choir. As the Society started its practices, the membership fee was fixed at 5/- (25p), honorary members paid 10/6d (52½p) and received two tickets at 3/- (15p) or three tickets at 2/- (10p) for each concert. On 13 December, with "over one hundred performers" the *Hiawatha* selection was presented. Members of the Layton family again joined the concert – Mr Alfred Layton (bass) from London, who sang for his son in 1910, and this time Mr Gilbert Layton, although his relationship cannot be identified but was probably a brother of the conductor, was the orchestra accompanist. Bach's *Magnificat* was planned for March, 1912, but when the rehearsals started in St Andrew's Church Schoolrooms, this was changed to Schubert's *Song of Miriam*. At the March concert in the Public Hall, moved from its original planned date by one week because of a clash with another musical group, Bach's *God so loved the World* had been added and Miss Layton returned as soloist. Numerical deficiency of tenors was again commented upon by the 'Paignton Observer and Echo' columnist. During the interval of the concert, Mr and Mrs Layton received presentations and, although not stated, it appears their departure was imminent if not immediate.

Ominously, as 1912 drew to a close, and as this history progresses into 1913, the local newspapers began to feature the problems in Europe leading to the First World War. During the year, on 15 April, another headline dominated the news for several weeks with the sinking of the one-and-a-quarter million pound White Star liner 'Titanic'.

By late 1913, editorial comments were being made about the lack of interest from men, and possibly a conductor, to reverse the demise of the Choral Society, yet again. Even the Orchestral Society had become dormant. At the end of the year in December, Mr Benson, who had been appointed joint conductor of the Society with Mr Harris in 1905-6 and who also played in local orchestras, wrote to the 'Paignton Observer and Echo' about the absence of choral concerts in Paignton. He observed under four headings that: there was apathy amongst male voices; oratorio was expensive; apathy of the public; counter attractions. He added "we have to charge three shillings (15p) for a seat when a better one may be had in the Torquay Pavilion generally for one shilling (5p)". He ended by stating that "if anything is done to alter this state of things, arrangements must be made to relieve the Conductor of all financial and business worries". In the same edition, the author of the 'Lucubration' column applauded Mr Benson's comments and ended his piece by stating "we shall feel it our duty to harp on the subject until a change for the better is forthcoming". Unfortunately, things did not change for the better, and in another way became tragically far worse with the outbreak of war on 5 August, 1914, and men drafted into the service of their country. However, just before the start of the war in April, 1914, Mr Harris appeared to have revived music with the Paignton New Opera Company, which is said to have sprung out of the Juvenile Operetta Society, performing Edward Solomon's *Billy Taylor*. The concert extended over three days with a Wednesday matinee and evening performance, Thursday evening and a further show in Brixham.

During the four years of the war some performances at the Public Hall, Paignton, continued with visiting celebrities billed. Oldway Mansion, Paignton, the Singers' home, with a capacity of up to two hundred and staffed by English, and for a time American, nurses, was used for the repatriation of wounded soldiers as they returned from the European Fronts. In Oldway a section was also provided as an American Women's War Hospital. As stretcher cases arrived by train, members of the local Fire Brigade were used as stretcher bearers with "ambulance cars and private motors requisitioned to assist". Another building used by the Choral Society in the twenty-first century, Torquay Assembly Hall, described at the time as "the large hall of the new Town Hall", was also used as a hospital ward.

Public Hall 1900's, now the Palace Avenue Theatre.

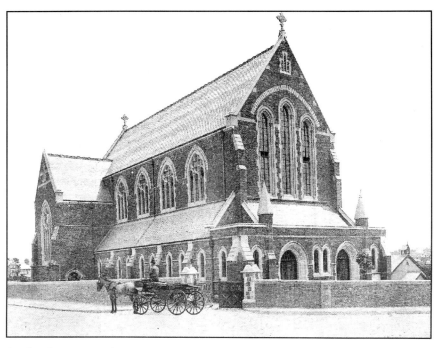

Christ Church, Paignton – early 1900's.

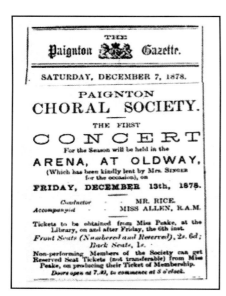

Original copy of the advertisement for the first concert –1878.

Logo the South Devon Choir adopted in 2001.

Paignton Choral Society, "Messiah" performance – May 26th, 1937.

Paignton Public Hall, Palace Avenue. Performance of "Hiawatha" – 1st May, 1968.

Central Church, Torquay, opened in 1976.

Christmas Carol Concert, English Riviera Centre – 15th December, 1988.

Quimper Cathedral, France – 17th August, 1989.

Performance of Vivaldi's "Gloria" in a church on the outskirts of Caen –
3rd May, 1999.

Publicity photograph at Paignton URC Hall – 2006.

Unique performance of "Carmina Burana" – Barnstable Pannier Market –
20th May, 2007.

"French Christmas" performance at Christ Church, Paignton – 29th
November, 2008.

Visiting Mini Minstrels Choir for Rutter's "Mass of the Children" – 5th December, 2009.

A typical rehearsal of South Devon Choir – Hollacombe CRC – 2010.

Audience assembling for a performance in Torquay Town Hall from the choir stalls.

Mozart concert performance at Central Church, Torquay – 16th April, 2011.

Chapter 2
1918-1939

AT THE START of this book a few facts of background information were provided to set the scene of the time, 1871. As we move into 1918, some up-dated information is now provided. King George VI was the Monarch with David Lloyd-George as Prime Minister. An 8lb (just over 3½ kg) loaf of bread cost between 1/3d and 1/4d (6p); railway bookings offered three classes (first, second and third, although the latter was not available on the express train); a complete set of dentures cost between £4 and £10; whisky could be purchased at 18/- per gallon (40p for 4½ litres) and tea between 2/- and 3/4d (10p to 17p). A comparison is again drawn between the prices listed and wages of the time: a teacher £500pa; agricultural worker £1.10.6 pw (£1.52½p); engineer 10/- per day (50p); shop assistant (male) £2.10.0 pw (£2.50p); shop assistant (female) £1.7.9 (£1.39p).

So we move on to 1919. Following the devastating loss of life, particularly men during the 1914-1918 war, attempts were made to return to normal life. The first rumblings to re-establish a Choral Society were heard in January of that year. Much of the information in the coming pages was obtained from the 'Paignton Observer & Echo', which gave good prominence to the Choral Section, and then to the Paignton Musical Association which was subsequently formed in the next few years. It is also noted that the 'Torquay Times' rarely, if ever, referred to either organization. It should also be borne in mind that all this happened at a time, in the following months, when considerable political unrest and national strikes took place, particularly by coal miners.

In a leader dated 16 January, 1919, in the 'Paignton Observer & Echo', the Paignton University Extension Society, which had just held its Victory Ball, was praised for its "intellectual feasts" of literary subjects and was asked to consider the arts, "the art of arts – music". Two weeks later at the AGM of that Society, chaired by Mr Arthur James, local Justice of the Peace, a Musical or Operatic Society was proposed with a sub-committee formed to draw up schemes and report back to the general committee. The large sub-committee for the Musical Section included Mr Benson, who was Joint Conductor with Mr Harris, 1905-6, and Mr Herbert Rushton, both mentioned later in this chapter, and Mr Harris, who played such a prominent role in the past and future success of the Paignton Choral Society.

Three weeks later, the 'Paignton Observer & Echo' warned that the first presentation of the choral group "should not be of too ambitious a nature, but a work pleasing to performers and listeners". For the next twelve months the subject of a choral society did not appear in the press at all. A reason for this might be the uncertainty of a suitable venue at which performances could be given, as the Public Hall owners were subject to liquidation procedures.

On Thursday, 19 June, 1919, at 2.00pm, the sea-end of the Paignton Pier and the Pavilion, although the latter was never used by the Choral Society as far as can be traced, was destroyed by fire. Up to that time the Pavilion regularly hosted concerts and other events and its loss was a major set-back for the entertainment world locally. Although insured and owned by the Devon Dock & Steamship Company, the local press following the story of the fire encouraged the District Council to buy the Pier, with the suggested possibility of extending its length and building a band stand on it. Along with other proposals this debate continued, at various times, right up to the start of World War II. In the meantime, over that period the ravages of the sea on the derelict structure caused further, serious, deterioration with local people describing it as an 'eye-sore'. It was purchased several times by various individuals who had plans to develop the Pier, and an ambitious design to erect a 'roofed-in-hall' at the shore-end was submitted. This plan was rejected by the Council as it would "block the view of the Bay infinitely more than building further out". The same month, the local Free Church Council, with a petition of two thousand five hundred signatures, objected to the opening of the Pier amusements on a Sunday which, it was claimed, was a flagrant breaking of the Sunday Observance Act. In a debate it was stated that the people who went there were principally from "the lower class who came to Paignton for their holidays"!

Some further space is now devoted to the other main and important venue for entertainment, the Public Hall. It was used frequently by the Choral Society over the next period 1921-1939, and a further forty-two years after the Second World War, during which it became to be known as the Palace Avenue Theatre. In March, 1919, the Directors of the Hall agreed to a sale to the Paignton Urban District Council, but administrative delays for the Council to borrow money from the Local Government Board resulted in a film company offering £1000 more on the asking price. However, the failure of the company to meet the deadline date in the contract, presumably because of the finance, enabled the Council to make a successful offer by 1920, although the price had gone up from £4,250 to £5,500. Shortly after the purchase had been completed, the local press was campaigning for enlargement of the floor accommodation, stage and dressing rooms and the added luxury of central heating. Use of the Bijou Theatre at the Gerston Hotel, referred to in Chapter 1 of this book and now described as an "Assembly Hall", had declined because of the extensive use of the Public Hall for a variety of events.

An attempt in May, 1920, was made by Mr. Leonard Mott to re-establish the Paignton Orchestral Society. It was previously run, very effectively before the War, by that now familiar name, Mr. Harris, Choirmaster and Organist at the Paignton Parish Church and earlier Conductor of the Paignton Choral Society.

During August, 1920, after several visits by Welsh Male Voice Choirs to the area, action was again urged for the provision of a choral and opera programme in the Autumn months. It was thought, however, that a "paucity" of young male voices would be experienced. The 'Paignton Observer & Echo' columnist described them as being interested in the "bawling of choruses and comic songs" and not in the "beauties of artistic singing such as the Welsh choirs show us"! He further commented on the absence of young men in church choirs, saying that many Paignton churches relied on choristers of "the old brigade" with over forty years singing record behind them.

Finally, on 7 September, 1920, the Paignton Musical Association was formed with Choral, Operatic and Orchestral Sections. The Dramatic part of the partnership did not start until the following year. Mr Robert Waycott was elected as Chairman of the Association. He was the son of Arthur Waycott, former organist at the Parish Church and also a local Estate Agent, Furnisher and Funeral Undertaker. This established business of Estate Agents is still in existence today, although the furniture and undertaking side of the business ceased in the early 1900's. Twenty days later the first rehearsal of the Choral Section since the start of World War I was held in the Gerston Assembly Room. Members were asked to pay an annual subscription of 5/- (25p). Mr. Harris once again took over the role of Conductor. He was to be assisted by Mr Benson, who also conducted the Orchestral Section. It was decided that Bennett's *May Queen* would be performed and music scores at 2/- (10p) were made available for purchase. This work had been sung by the Society in Paignton in January, 1887, and was described as having "goish choruses". It is interesting to record that the rehearsal venue was the Assembly Room in the Gerston Hall, which also housed the Bijou Theatre, famous for that first production of Gilbert and Sullivan's *Pirates of Penzance* in 1879.

The *May Queen* was performed on 19 December, 1920, in the Public Hall with "glees and songs". Unfortunately, the Conductor, Mr. Harris, was ill some days prior to the concert and Mr. Benson conducted the evening. Tickets were priced at 3/- (15p) and 2/- (10p) with unreserved seats at 1/6d (7½p). One of the four soloists was a Mademoiselle Fifine de la Cote who first sang in a Paignton concert at the age of fifteen and was now described as amongst the first flight of English sopranos. Two other soloists were a husband and wife, Mr. Norman Bickle (baritone) and Mrs

Bickle (contralto) with the tenor Mr. Alfred Wills. The chorus, it was reported, numbered over one hundred with a forty-strong orchestra.

The attraction of the cinema as competition with live theatre and music will be mentioned later in this chapter. It is noted that one cinema in Paignton, The Picture House, at this time advertised that balcony seats could be purchased at 15/- (75p) for a book of ten tickets. All performances included an orchestra. At 1/6d (7½p) a seat this price was quite competitive, and even attractive, against the Choral Section's price above.

The success of the concert in December led to a decision by the Committee to perform, the following Easter, *Hiawatha's Wedding Feast*. The Secretary of the Section made a public request to purchase or loan second-hand copies of the score. With the imminent performance on 13 April, 1921, the formation of the Operatic Section of the Musical Association was being sought by Flaneur in the 'Paignton Observer & Echo'. Part of an interesting article is quoted here and this may provoke and even irritate readers of this book and choral singers: "The fear that opera will tend to kill the choral section is an entirely groundless one. We would suggest holding the respective performances at different seasons, so as to obviate any such possibility; but beyond, and above that, there is only room for the cast in an opera, whereas a choral class can contain as many as desired – the more, the merrier. Picked voices, and for the most part young people, are required for operas; we thank our stars the grey hairs do not preclude one from doing one's bit in the choral section"!

Attendance at the Spring *Hiawatha's Wedding* concert, again in the Public Hall, was affected by many counter attractions. The performance appears, however, to have been appreciated by the audience with Mr Benson again conducting the Choir as Mr. Harris was still indisposed. It is also noted that the event took place at a time when the miners' strike was still taking hold on the country. A newspaper Public Notice stated that an Emergency Power had been provoked under a 1920 Act of Parliament. No electricity was permitted to be used for advertisements or display and fuel-rationing for coal was imposed. Misuse of gas or electricity could mean that an abuser might have his supply cut off!

Five days later, after the *Hiawatha* concert on the 18 April, at a meeting in the Badminton Hall, the Music Association appointed an Executive Committee to restart an Operatic Section. As stated earlier, it was felt that the Choral Section would be unaffected by this as there was room for both in the Association. By Autumn the Dramatic Section, the last arm which had been planned by the parent-body, was created, although for some reason there was a delay and it did not start meeting until November, 1922. It appears that the three Sections, with varying degrees of continuity, were later incorporated into the new subsequent organization the Paignton Operatic, Dramatic and Choral Society after the Second World War.

In September, 1921, Mr. Benson withdrew from conducting the Choral Section and it appears that Mr. Harris had also resigned, probably due to continuing bad health. Mr. Herbert Rushton, Organist at St Matthew's Church, Cockington, Torquay, stepped into the post of Conductor of both the Choral and Operatic Sections of the Musical Association. It was felt that with a population which had now risen to 14,000 in Paignton, the Association had a bright future.

Rehearsals, it is noted, had now moved to the YMCA Gymnasium in Palace Avenue, Paignton, where practices for *Hiawatha's Departure* were due to commence. The following January this work was performed at the Choral Section's established concert venue, the Public Hall, with a smaller chorus than at previous concerts. The first cry by the Choral Section since its start after the war was heard for male singers. Had the start of the Operatic Section already had its effect on these numbers or was there some other reason? The newspaper in the 'Paignton Observer & Echo' stated that twenty-five years earlier there was "half the population" in Paignton yet "more tenors than today". Five times as many basses were also available compared to those who took part in the concert. Despite this lack of men, at a Whist Drive organized by the Musical Association in the famous Deller's Café – the social meeting place in Paignton for meals including afternoon tea, often with a pianist playing – it was stated by the Choral Section's Secretary that they hoped to hold two concerts in the coming year.

An advertisement in the 'Paignton Observer & Echo' stated that the rehearsals for the concert version of *Tom Jones* would commence in September, 1922. Thirteen days before Christmas the work was performed and was described as a true and genuine success. An additional comment was made in the newspaper that rehearsals had been slightly reduced because of the General Election and "other distractions" and that a work of that nature needed careful rehearsing before a performance was given to the public. Within a month Mr. Rushton was conducting the Operatic Section's concerts of the *Mikado* over a period of five days. In what to an outsider may seem like a whirlwind life, on Monday, 5 February, 1923, the same Conductor started rehearsals for Haydn's *Creation* with the Choral Section. In the same month Mr. Harris suffered a personal loss when his wife suddenly died. A 'Paignton Observer & Echo' article stated that she also had musical talent like her husband, and was well known in musical circles. It stated that her "orchestra frequently played at local gatherings".

Four months later, in May, the first two parts of *Creation* were advertised as having a "large chorus" and "augmented orchestra". Part II of this work had previously been performed by the Society in May, 1910, in the Public Hall. Unfortunately, only a moderate-sized audience attended with, this time, the lateness of the season blamed as the reason. The Executive Committee stated that it had been forced to accept a later date for the concert although no reason for this can be traced. The advertised large chorus appears to conflict with the 'Paignton Observer & Echo' review, which said "one would like to have seen the chorus seats more fully occupied".

On the 2 October, 1923, Mr. Percy Pearse held a meeting to form a Paignton Male Voice Choir. Whilst welcoming a male voice choir in the town, the local newspaper commented "there will be a rare old stirring of the dry bones if enough men are to form a choir" and that the promoters need to "walk warily"! If the Choir did get off the ground there was a warning that it could affect the Choral Society male sections. However, in reality, it appears that it was necessary to hold a further meeting six months later asking all interested to attend. No follow-up report can be traced to state whether this invitation was successful in finding sufficient singers at that stage.

At the AGM in September, 1923, the Vicar of Paignton Parish Church, Rev H Mackworth Drake, who had been inducted in June 1920 to the Parish, was re-elected as President of the Paignton Choral Society. This title of the Choir seems to have crept into articles over the previous twelve months and it is not clear whether this was a newspaper initiative or whether the Choral Section was striving for independence from the Musical Association. The latter was certainly to come about just under sixty years later! To return to the AGM, the work AR Gaul's *Joan of Arc* was selected for the next concert, this having been performed at the Birmingham Festival some years earlier by another choir. The concert in December, 1923, was well received again by a "moderate audience" and accompanied by that now familiar cry, more males needed. In the 'Paignton Observer & Echo', the critic Flaneur, was rather damning in his comments when he stated that he considered the concert had been a rather "immature production" with insufficient time allowed for practice. He felt that, added to this, the "slackness on the part of the public" to attend could have been attributed to the aftermath of the General Election and the "lack of acquaintance with the kind of work to be performed".

In 1924 a long debate started about the Public Hall and this was to rumble on right up to the start of World War II. With a massive bill of just over £71,000 for sewerage and water improvements, the Paignton Urban District Council could not find the money for a replacement Hall. Complaints about the stage size, heating and dressing room accommodation were frequently raised by the public. For example, regarding dressing rooms, the men had to scale a ladder to gain access to the garret room in which to change. Greater use of the Hall and a rising population also presented problems. Following inclement weather one planned major outdoor event had to be moved into the Hall. Contrary to the law, the doors had to be locked, to prevent some of the capacity crowd from entering as the Hall was already full. A short holiday season, determining a suitable location and what departments should be accommodated in a new building were all deterrents for a replacement. Local councillors had already expressed the view to Flaneur that provision of a new building might be provided "after we are dead" and that at present "not a penny-piece will be spent on that place" (the Public Hall).

To return to the Choral Society (as it will now be referred to, although still part of the Music Association), a General Meeting was held on 24 March, 1924, to see whether the Society should continue with any degree of success. A debt of £80.12.4 (£80.62), the shortage of men and poor audience attendance were all presenting problems. A resolution was passed unanimously that the Society should continue with a social evening in the hope of wiping out the debt. One month later, stating that the population of Paignton had now risen to 15,000, the 'Paignton Observer & Echo' reporter proposed that a popular oratorio should be chosen, as he felt that the previous work performed had been an "obscure production". It seems that this advice did not fall on deaf ears, and *Elijah* was selected for the next performance. Rehearsals commenced in October with, apparently, only thirty to forty singers. Mr Rushton remained as Conductor, but during the time of the Operatic Section's rehearsals and performance Mr Harris took over the Choral Society's rehearsals. On 4 April, 1925, two concerts were given, one in the afternoon and the other in the evening. These were highly acclaimed, with a good-sized choir and audience in attendance. On 8 May, 1925, the Annual Meeting was held and members were told that funds appeared to have taken a modest turn for the better, with "four to five shillings" in hand (20p to 25p)! Membership had risen from sixty-four in the previous year to over one hundred.

The Choral Society chose to perform *Messiah* for their March, 1926, concert and rehearsals commenced in October the previous year at the YMCA. A matinee and evening concert were given in the Public Hall to a fairly large audience on each occasion and the performances were described as "meritorious" in one report and an "unquestionable triumph" in another. Slight confusion exists between a report in the 'Paignton Observer & Echo', which stated that the Public Hall was used, but the 'Western Guardian' refers to the Paignton Co-operative Hall'. Quite where the latter name originates is uncertain! However, by the date of the concert, the long-awaited central heating had been installed.

In April, 1926, Mr Rushton extended his skills in another direction by forming the Paignton Orchestral Society which was "for practice and performance of music etc, and to assist the Operatic, Dramatic and Choral

Societies and others requiring help". It was suggested that this could become the fourth arm of the Musical Association.

A month later, at the Choral Society's AGM, the Executive Committee reported that the finances were good – in excess of £7. Gounod's *Redemption* was to be presented, although a question of royalties had to be sorted out. Rehearsals, it appeared, had now moved to the Elementary School in Curledge Street, Paignton. It was suggested that young males were not taking the trouble to develop their voices because the "somewhat inane attraction of jazz, cinemas and motor bikes carry too many guns for the study of the art of arts". This was followed in the newspaper with praise for the Paignton Male Voice Choir formed in the style of the previous Paignton Orpheus Choir. The reader may recall that attempts were made to start it in 1923 and by 1925, from humble beginnings of nine or ten members, it had risen to twenty-eight with a limit imposed on a membership of thirty-six. It was further stated in the article that the "Male Voice Choir had not been unattended with great difficulties to one cause and this may be attributed to one of the facts that Devon generally is not a musical county". In December, 1926, it was reported that the Choir seemed "destined to be a nursery for the Choral and Operatic male choruses". How the Male Voice Choir members viewed this comment at the time is not known!

In July the 'Paignton Observer & Echo' printed its first-ever photograph. This development in newspaper technology would be used to considerable advantage by many organizations and people, not least the Operatic and Dramatic Sections to advertise character parts played by their members in forthcoming productions. The photograph in this instance was Lillie Seldon and her Jazz Band Cabaret in the 'Piccadilly Follies' performing at the Adelphi Gardens in Paignton.

In February, 1927, the Operatic Society's performance of *Les Cloches de Corneville* received disappointing audiences. The profits for the Monday and Tuesday performances were to have been donated to the local hospital. In fact, there was a deficit and the donation was not possible. The Operatic Society was also now suffering from a lack of male voices.

On 12 April, 1927, temporary disaster struck. The lack of male voices, particularly tenors, made it impossible for the Choral Society to tackle the work proposed and the performance was postponed. Change of the rehearsal location, the practice day and illness were all considered the main reasons why attendance had fallen. Flaneur, who was still championing local music, questioned the wisdom of the choice of the work *Redemption* for the next concert. The question is posed as to whether the success of the Paignton Male Voice Choir, mentioned previously, affected both the Operatic and Choral Society's male numbers.

With rehearsals due to start again in October, it was announced on 22 September that an organ recital at the Paignton Parish Church would be given the following Wednesday by Dr Harold Rhodes, organist at St John's Church, Torquay. The proceeds of the event, organized by the Paignton Parish Choir, were to be given to Mr Frank Harris, who was seriously ill in a London Hospital. It will be remembered that he had been Conductor of the Paignton Choral Society at various times over twenty-six years as well as organist and choirmaster of the Parish Church for forty-three years. Sadly, the arranged concert was to be overshadowed by his death, at the age of sixty-nine, on the day of the concert. It was decided to go ahead with a suitably modified programme.

By October, 1927, a specially-convened AGM considered, amongst other matters, whether the Choral Society's activities should be left in abeyance. The lack of male voices was mentioned for the umpteenth time. Overtures had been made by the Secretary at a meeting with the Male Voice Choir to persuade some of their members to join the Choral Society, but a response had been given that "many were married men and they had two practices a week already". It was also reported that some Choral Society members had been lost to another unnamed Torquay society. Mr Rushton, the Conductor, thanked the ladies "who had always supported the Society but it was the men who let them down"! With a new organist to be appointed to the Parish Church, it was hoped that he might fill the position of Conductor which Mr Rushton was now relinquishing. On 13th December, from a list of fifty to sixty applicants for the post of Parish Organist and Choirmaster, three candidates were shortlisted. They each in turn took choir practice and Mr Leonard Baggaley, Deputy Organist at Ripon Cathedral, was eventually appointed. Prior to the Cathedral post he had been Deputy Organist and Choirmaster at a church in Nottingham and also organist to the Choral Society in that city. He played the organ for the first time in his new appointment at the 1927 Christmas Day services.

Over the next five months Flaneur continued to press for the revival of the Choral Society and to suggest that the newly appointed Organist at the Parish Church should take over the conductorship. An appeal for assistance from their large body of tenors and basses was repeated to the Male Voice Choir and Operatic Society. As pressure built, a General Meeting was called in July, the outcome of which led to the proposal that Mr Baggaley be appointed as Conductor. Stanford's *Revenge* was chosen as the work to perform. Rehearsals did not in fact start until October and the number of singers attending, especially men, was disappointing.

One year later, by the end of 1929, there was no sign on the horizon of a concert being performed. Ironically, the Paignton Male Voice Choir was giving successful concerts. It was even stated in the 'Paignton Observer & Echo' that the Choir consisted of forty male voices (they had obviously lifted their upper limit previously agreed) and a "nursery" had been started. Members of this would be "instructed in the rudiments of music so that as vacancies occur in the main choir, they are filled by a singer already prepared for the class of work that confronts him"! It is also noted that at a Mozart performance given by the Parish Choir, new candlesticks were dedicated in the Church in memory of Mr Harris.

Mr Baggaley, appointed in 1927, had already taken up the baton for the Paignton Operatic Society and conducted a memorable event over the last two days of December 1929 and New Year's day, 1930, with matinee and evening performances on the 2 and 3 of January. The event was the *Pirates of Penzance*, marking the jubilee of the premiere performance in Paignton, and in Britain, of the Gilbert and Sullivan work. The Bijou Theatre, part of the Gerston Hotel and mentioned in Chapter 1, was where the initial performance had taken place and was now used again, although the Theatre had been converted into bedrooms. For this special event the stage area was restored, dressing room accommodation provided and a special box in the auditorium placed where it had been used by the late Mr Dendy, the Paignton entrepreneur referred to in the early pages of Chapter 1.

The doldrums continued for the Choral Society well into 1930, despite several articles in the local paper advocating action. In November it was again suggested that the Male Voice Choir should volunteer their services to help. It was felt that it might provide a nucleus of male voices and that "some musical enthusiast will stir the dry bones of the present executive and get to work with some form of choral music".

Returning to May of that year (1930), a piece in the 'Paignton Observer & Echo' caught the eye of the author of this book. It was reported that, at the Torquay Music Festival in the Pavilion, Torquay, the Municipal Orchestra was conducted on a Thursday by Sir Henry Wood and the following day by Sir Edward Elgar who was conducting some of his own compositions. This stirred Flaneur to suggest that it was high time Paignton had its own orchestra and hinted that a festival-type event should be held locally. Four years later in October, the Festival in Torquay was to attract Sir Henry Wood back as Conductor in the opening concert and two days later Doctor, known then as Mr Adrian Boult, took the stage in the same capacity.

Earlier in the year of 1931, the national census showed that the population of Paignton had increased from 14,451 in 1921 to 18,405. Maybe this prompted the idea in June, 1931, for a new Society to be formed known as the 'Paignton New Choral Society'. A prominent townsman and councillor, Mr Geoffrey Spanton, was appointed as President with Mr Baggaley as Conductor. With rehearsals starting in October, the original thought of performing Stanford's *Revenge* was resurrected. This hope was short-lived. It appears that for the next six years the 'New Society' faded into oblivion. It is impossible at the time of writing this history to ascertain whether members continued to meet socially or rehearse set works. Flaneur seemed to have given up all mention of a Choral Society in his column, possibly because of sheer frustration. Probably some members augmented other choirs or the Operatic Section of the Musical Association. The success of *Messiah* in Torquay Pavilion in December, 1931, was attributed in the 'Paignton Observer and Echo' to several Paigntonians who participated. However, it appeared that in Torquay and Paignton choral music productions were suffering financially, which was attributed to the stress of the time with massive national unemployment and poverty in many sections of the community.

To keep my readers' attention, it was thought that some other items pertinent to the local music scene, but not necessarily in chronological order, might be of interest. Much of the information was gained still through the local 'Paignton Observer & Echo'. However, in addition to the 'Western Guardian', which repeated most of the former newspaper's information, a new paper for the town came on sale, the 'Paignton News and Brixham & Preston Chronicle'.

From June, 1929, as mentioned earlier, the Paignton Urban District Council debated the subject of the Public Hall on many occasions, and the 'Paignton Observer & Echo' added more fuel to the fire concerning the inadequacies and cramped accommodation of the said venue. With the building having outgrown its usefulness, a new "glass-covered pavilion, a summer building where band concerts could be held in ideal conditions whatever the state of the weather outside may be", was amongst the suggestions put forward. Three years later an even more ambitious idea was created for a hall with a seating capacity for one thousand, seven hundred and twenty. An alternative idea was also mooted to demolish the Public Hall and build a modern building on the site for a concert theatre, library and offices for the Council which were scattered around the town. Needless to say, the matter was not carried forward. (Sounds familiar with the recent ideas considered at one stage by the Torbay Council in 2010 and since dropped.)

In the same year, whilst the Choral Society "slept", once described during a previous doldrum period as "asleep but not dead", the Paignton Male Voice Choir continued with successful appearances at concerts and functions. However, it is reported that their April concert in that year attracted very poor attendance. The following month the Choir was awarded the Silver Challenge Cup for Male Voice Choirs at the Torquay Eisteddfod, and in September it was described as the "Premier Choir" in the newspaper headlines, achieving first/second place in the "sextette" and "quartette" categories at the Newton Abbot Eisteddfod. The previous year the Male Voice Choir had been in danger of collapsing when their Conductor, Mr Percy Pearse, resigned owing to ill-health. Mr L Thomas kept the Choir going for a while until the Deputy Conductor, Mr T Williams took over the conductorship resulting in the Choir returning to its previous high standard as indicated earlier.

In June, 1933, following a public meeting in April, the Chairman of the Council, Mr George Kingdon, chaired a meeting, when it was proposed that Paignton should have its own event – the Paignton Music Festival. The idea emanated from Mr Thomas of the Paignton Male Voice Choir. A suggestion at the meeting was made that the Festival might be combined with the Torquay Music Festival, but this was strongly rejected by him. He stated that it should be run by Paignton people, and went on to say: "people in the Midlands had not heard of Paignton. Some knew it was near Torquay. Paignton needed to be known as Paignton and not a suburb of Torquay". Mr Richard Harris, who ran a local wireless (radio) business in Paignton, was appointed Chairman of the Executive Committee, which included other prominent figures in the community. September, 1934, was planned for the Festival to be held, but the headmaster of the local boys' school pointed out that this would prevent schools from participating. The timing, therefore, was changed to November and held over a period of three days.

Many audiences travelled to concerts by various means, probably including trams, which had been running since 17 July, 1811, between Torquay and Paignton. In November, 1932, a debate started as to whether that form of transport should be replaced by trolley-buses. After considerable controversy when both Paignton Urban District Council and Torquay Corporation opposed the plans on grounds of expenditure, the plan was dropped. The last tram ran from Torquay to Paignton on 7 January, 1934. Other trams were still operating in parts of Torquay the following month. The Torquay-to-Paignton journey was replaced by a fleet of four buses which ran every five minutes during week-days.

An additional item which occurred in June, 1933 should be added here. After a long absence, through illness, the Rev Mackworth Drake, President of the Paignton Music Association, returned to the Parish Church for the Harvest Festival Service. He had been away since the Sunday before Easter (8 April) with severe blood poisoning in his arm. In fact his ill-health had taken its toll and two years later in September, 1935, he gave his last sermon after nearly fifteen and a half years as Vicar. He moved subsequently to the quieter parish of Berry Pomeroy as Vicar. A month later, Rev Basil Dale, the youngest ever Vicar in the Parish at the age of thirty-two, was inducted and gave his first sermon in January, 1936. Twelve months later he became President of the Choral Society.

By 1934, in the Public Hall ("why don't they change that dreary title?" the 'Paignton News' satirical reporter asked) a new proscenium area with lighting had been provided for the opening of the Repertory Theatre season. Further improvements had been made in preparation for Paignton's first pantomime on Boxing Day in 1935. In praise of the work carried out by the Council, the 'Paignton News' had a hilarious article about the 'improvements' which is partially quoted here: "The old proscenium complete with those supporting 'marble' pillars – more like rolls of linoleum –has completely vanished. And so, it is hoped, has the murderous 'wall of death' red curtain which has so often nearly put an end to some of our local talent as it descended with a mad rush at the finale". The change in size of the proscenium gave extra room back-stage. However, the writer went on to say: "I trust that awful vision of a 'forest' backcloth that suddenly bulges and sways most distressingly at the most dramatic moments as some of the cast endeavour to get across the stage to make an entrance" had gone. The columnist's final remarks are just as amusing: "But our next move is to make the life of councillors unbearable until they agree to spend a few pounds on making the exterior of the Hall more suitable as a place of entertainment and less like the back approach to a warehouse". In September, 1935, another revised pavilion plan for a winter garden, restaurant and town building designed by a local young architect appeared in the 'Paignton Observer & Echo', with the cost now at £80,000. The seating capacity had been revised to twelve hundred and fifty and it was suggested that to spread the cost the building could be erected in stages.

Dwelling for the moment on 1935, preparations for the Silver Jubilee Celebration on 6 May for King George V and Queen Mary dominated the news most of the weeks prior to the date. A march-past to and from the Parish Church and gun salute in the morning, tea parties for the children in the afternoon and an evening performance in the Public Hall of the "Paignton Pudding" were all planned. With one hundred and fifty performers, the latter was to depict the principle events during the reign of the King and Queen portrayed by some Operatic, Dramatic and, one suspects, the Choral Section members. The whole day was rounded off with fireworks and the lighting of a bonfire beacon. Although all the events were reported in the local newspapers, no mention was made of the theatrical performance, which may have lacked support and was abandoned. Tragically on the 20 January, 1936, the King died and further turmoil in Royal circles occurred when King Edward VIII, who succeeded King George but was never crowned, abdicated on 10 December in the same year. His brother Albert, using his last name George, succeeded him two days later to become King George VI.

Referring back directly to the entertainment scene between 1932 and 1936, the Operatic Society gave a number of what are described as "brilliant performances" but with mixed financial fortunes. Whilst some houses had full audiences, others had poor attendance. In January, 1933, *My Lady Molly* was sparsely attended with half-full houses with the result that two hundred tickets were given away to the unemployed for the Friday and Saturday performances in an endeavour to fill the empty seats. All this was probably a reflection of the economic situation of the time with mass unemployment for some sections of the community. For those not affected, the expanding popularity of other sources of entertainment was becoming an increasing threat. The 'Paignton Picture House' described as "the Picture House between the Station and the sea" in Torbay Road (still in existence today as one of the oldest cinemas in the country although closed to the public for many years) was showing films regularly. In August, 1932, the 'Regent' in Station Square (now a small supermarket with flats above) and the 'Palladium' (demolished and flats erected on the site at the entrance to Oldway Mansion) were also in competition with the live theatre. They offered comfortable upholstered seats compared to the canvas seats with upright backs used for audiences in the Public Hall. Further, on Good Friday in 1934, despite the fact of rejection on previous occasions, the cinemas were granted a special licence to open on that day. There was considerable opposition from the Church to this sanction. Contrary to this religious condemnation, approval was given by the Magistrates, who stated that the cinemas must not open before 5.45pm with the film starting at 6.00pm. A synopsis of the films, which had to be classified 'U' and which the Bench stated must not be "objectionable", had to be provided to the local Superintendent of Police. The following year the local Magistrates agreed to the same terms with a further statement that the "films must be chosen discreetly". Generally, with the films of the time starring Charlie Chaplin, Clarke Gable, Marlene Dietrich, Gertrude Lawrence and "glorious technicolour" film of the Coronation celebrations, the public had counter attractions. Flaneur in May, 1936, was already warning: "it is no disputing it, the cinema is the modern form of entertainment. It has killed the theatre and put other forms of entertainment into the shade".

In the previous four years the Dramatic Section was very active, as was Mr Baggaley. In December, 1933, a copy of the 'Paignton Observer & Echo' stated that the Operatic Society due to perform *Floradora* was seeking sopranos, unlike the Choral Society, which always seemed to be lacking tenors. In March, 1934, Mr Baggaley made his debut as Musical Director of the Operatic Society and also the similar society in Brixham. Later he became Conductor of the Torquay Orchestral Society. He was already the Music Master at Marist Convent School in Paignton (since closed) which each year performed public concerts. It will be remembered that all this was in addition to his duties as Parish Organist and Choirmaster. In August, 1934, presentations were made to Mr Martin, who retired after thirty years' service as Organist and Choirmaster at Christ Church, Paignton. He had also been Joint Conductor with Mr Harris of the Choral Society from 1885 to 1886.

By November, 1934, the Operatic Society may well have solved its problem of the lack of sopranos, but was now suffering the Choral Society's malady with an advertisement in the paper stating "Men Wanted!" for the forthcoming production of *The Arcadians* the following March. The reviews in the newspapers were glowing and stated that on several nights audiences were turned away because the house was full. Mr Baggaley was in charge of the musical side of Paignton's pantomime for many years and conducted at performances. *Babes in the Wood* was presented in the Public Hall from Boxing Day, 1935, to New Year's Day, 1936, with packed audiences. The earlier fears that audiences might abandon the live stage in favour of the cinema do not seem, for the moment, founded. In January, 1935, the 'Paignton Observer and Echo' reported that Mr Baggaley's skills as an organist had been recognized when he was awarded a Fellowship of the Royal College of Organists.

Unfortunately, local music activities were to suffer a blow in October, 1936, when Mr Baggaley apparently sprang a surprise on the Vicar and congregation of the Parish Church by announcing that he had accepted the post of Borough Organist for the Dover Corporation. The Paignton Operatic Society managed to appoint a new Musical Director, Mr Ernest Goss, the Torquay Corporation's Musical Director, General Manager of the Torquay Pavilion and Musical Director of the Torquay Municipal Orchestra. He took over this responsibility in November, 1936, in time for the preparation of the Golden Jubilee production of *The Maid of the Mountains*, performed over five days the following March.

In October, 1936, aged thirty-seven, Mr Gerald King, organist and Choirmaster at Glastonbury, succeeded Mr Baggaley as Paignton Parish Organist and Choirmaster. He carried out these duties throughout, and almost to the end of, World War II. Prior to this official start in the area of his duties in the Parish Church, he was involved as Musical Director of the orchestra, for the pantomime *Aladdin*, which was performed in 1936 in the Public Hall. By Autumn of the following year he had become Musical Director of the Operatic Societies in Paignton and Brixham, and was music teacher at the Marist Convent in Paignton. He also became Conductor of the Torbay Orchestra, which appears to have been an amalgam of the Paignton and Torquay Orchestral Societies.

Even more surprising, despite its having achieved so much success in the early 1930's, the Paignton Male Voice Choir officially disbanded on 19 March, 1936, after its winter concert in 1935. It was re-formed the following October as the "New Paignton Male Voice Choir" with Mr Pearse returning as the Honorary Conductor. The Committee decided to explore "the rural extension scheme of increasing musical knowledge in rural areas" in co-operation with Dartington Hall, Totnes, and the British Broadcasting Corporation. The Director of Music at Dartington Hall, Mr Ronald Biggs, expressed the opinion that the Male Voice Choir had the "material to become one of the best choirs in the West of England".

Hoorah! To return to the Choral Society once more – good news! As prime mover, Mr King, the new Parish Organist, arranged a meeting on Thursday, 17 January, 1937, to re-launch the Paignton Choral Society. Fifty people attended the event, at Deller's Café with the Curate-in-charge of St Andrew's Church, Paignton, Rev Harold Fores chairing the meeting and the Vicar of the Parish Church, Rev Basil Dale, appointed as President. A decision was made to perform *Messiah* soon after Easter. It appears that Mr King's enthusiasm for a Choral Society had led to his writing "several dozen letters to prospective members asking them to attend the inaugural meeting", so the 'Paignton News' reported. A subscription of 3d (about 1p) per week, excluding the Summer Holiday period, was accepted by the members at the meeting with voice tests imposed for singers who wished to join.

In writing a book over a historical period, it is possible for the author to foresee the future and to comment. Prior to the concert in 1937, a lecture had been given on the "necessity" of Air Raid Precautions by the Assistant Surgeon of the St John Ambulance Brigade. Subsequently, the Paignton Urban District Council at one of their meetings, suggested the need to appoint an Area Organiser for Air Raid Precautions. Funding for this evolved into a dispute between local councils and the government and the appointment was deferred. By early 1939 the growing threat of war appeared more imminent with the newspaper using such ominous words as "evacuees, gas masks, black-out, air raid precautions, sandbag filling, food and fuel rationing".

At this point a little more space is again, briefly, devoted to the Public Hall. In January, 1936, there had been an internal transformation making it a "brighter and cosier" place. Controversial debates had continued for the type of replacement hall which was needed, although a comment by a local Ratepayers' Association had been made that a pavilion in a seaside resort was "like an umbrella – it is handy when it is raining, otherwise it is a nuisance and frequently results in a loss to its owner". In April, 1937, the Operatic Section of the Paignton Musical Association visited Ashburton Town Hall for a Gilbert & Sullivan performance where they found "plush tip-up seats". The 'Paignton News' wanted to know why the Public Hall did not have them. A photograph of the time showed people sitting on beach-hut type canvas seats in an exhibition. However, by 1939 new seating had been installed at a cost of £425.

Amidst the celebration of the Coronation of King George VI at Westminster Abbey on 12 May, 1937, the *Messiah* concert was still given by the Choral Society on 26 May with a matinee and evening performance. It is interesting to note that inflation in those days must have been moderate. The price of tickets at 3/6d (17p), 2/6d (12½p), and 2/- (10p) reserved, with 1/6d (6p) and 9d (4p) unreserved compares favourably with the first performance after the war in 1920. The prices then were 3/- (15p), 2/- (10 p) reserved, 1/3d (6p) unreserved. The Society considered the possibility of making arrangements for unreserved special-price seats for schools to attend the matinee performance. Whether this offer was taken up is not recorded anywhere. A full orchestra of thirty players, with a chorus of one hundred singers, was advertised for the two performances in the Public Hall.

For the 1938 annual concert on 27 April, the first part of Coleridge-Taylor's *Bon Bon Suite,* with one hundred and twenty performers, was given. A miscellany of part-items and items and songs was included in the second half of the programme. The concert was conducted by a Guest Conductor, Mr Reginald Redman, the Musical Director of the West Regional Station of the BBC. It included some of his own compositions.

At Deller's Café, the same venue as the original meeting in January, 1937, to restart the Society, Mr King addressed the Rotary Club on 18 April. He was highly critical of the fact that, at that time in England, music was taking a back seat. He felt that areas varied, and whilst Paignton was as musical generally as most places, it suffered for a number of reasons. He said that the Public Hall, which again had been the subject of much debate and controversy regarding its replacement, was described as a draughty place for concert audiences with performing members practically having "to go on their bended knees to beg people to come and they had about a three hundred out of a population of about twenty thousand". Mr King blamed those people who preferred to listen to the wireless. He also thought that Paignton as a seaside resort had to look after visitors and their pockets. There was a "cinema religion" prevalent and a lazy attitude of Paigntonians to do anything musically for themselves. Words of wisdom – a month later it was reported that the *Messiah* concerts had made a loss!

By February, 1937, the Paignton Male Voice Choir was reported as having twenty-five members and six probationers. It appears that all members in the past session had had lectures on "all matters musical and at the end of the course took a written paper on questions relating to the lectures". An eighty per cent of marks, together with a voice test, were necessary to become full members of the Choir. The Choir was continuing its high standard by winning first place at the Torquay and Plymouth Music Festival, although Mr Pearse was indisposed and Mr Jago conducted on his behalf. The Operatic Section was still going strong, although the Dramatic Section within the Musical Association umbrella, was in a low period and "under a cloud".

In October *Elijah* rehearsals started for the Choral Society with plans for a performance in February, 1939, although warnings were again sounded about choir attendance and the need for more members. The concert, planned to take place in February, was given in March with a chorus and orchestra of one hundred and twenty, assisted by forty members from the Brixham Choral Society. The concert was well attended and received a favourable review which can be summed up in the 'Paignton News' quotation: "one went away with the desire to hear another oratorio by the Society in the not too distant future". This was not to be, as Britain entered the Second World War on 3 September, 1939, and on the 19 October the Paignton Choral Society suspended activity. It was felt that with the call-up of men for active service, the Choir numbers would be depleted. A suggestion at the general meeting was put forward that local choirs in the town might join forces. This was rejected, as it was felt that the combined group could not be called the Paignton Choral Society and therefore activity of that group must cease for the duration of the War. An £8 debt in the accounts was wiped out by a contribution from each member of 2/6d (12½p).

To end this chapter, it is worth noting two other items. At the AGM in November, 1939, despite the loss of good voices, the Paignton Male Voice Choir decided that it would continue its activities with membership standing at thirty-three – the same as at the annual meeting the previous years. However, another important project did become a casualty of the war. A sixtieth celebration in December, 1939, marking the first performance of the *Pirates of Penzance* at the Bijou Theatre on 30 December, 1879, was "rendered impossible" for the Paignton Operatic Society "because of the war".

The Choral Society was not to meet again until 1946 - well after the cessation of hostilities. During the war the Public Hall, which has been referred to so often on previous pages, was used as a Garrison Theatre for service personnel and civilians. Prior to the D-day landings American troops were entertained there.

Chapter 3
1946-1999

WORLD WAR II in Europe ended on 7 May, 1945, and in just over a year the Paignton Operatic, Dramatic and Choral Society recommenced its activities. At this time King George VI was Monarch, and following the first post-war General Election in 1945, Winston Churchill was defeated and Clement Atlee became Prime Minister. Legacies of war still remained with bread rationing, despite a good harvest, and petrol for use in cars was subject to coupon-use. Torquay United was half-way down Division 3 (South). For those gambling on the Football Pools, Vernons paid out £6,526.10.0 (£6526.50) for a 1d bet (less than 1p). In the entertainment world two stations were broadcast by the British Broadcasting Corporation, Home and Light programmes, and at local cinemas Greer Garson, Gregory Peck and the Marx Brothers were featuring in films. A three bedroom semi-detached bungalow could be bought for £3,250 freehold and a detached house for £500 more. To compare these figures with the wages of the time, a live-in cook was paid £2.10.0pw (£2.50) and a daily help £3.5.0pw (£3.25); a non-hospital night nurse was paid £12 monthly plus meals.

At the time when the Society group recommenced, the Inland Revenue Department defined the Society as a "commercial organization" and, therefore, all performances would be subject to an entertainment tax on money received from ticket sales. As a result of this, in order to avoid paying this tax, the Operatic Section decided that if a choral society was formed it would be deemed to be a "cultural organization", as would a dramatic society. Thus the Paignton Operatic, Dramatic and Choral Society was created on 3 October, 1946, although, as you will read later, this rather cumbersome organization became a thorn in the Choral Section's side. At the General Meeting officers were elected for each Section of the parent-group and the Choral Section appointed Dr A Fairburn Barnes as Honorary Conductor/Director of Music, a post he was to hold for the next ten years. The Chairperson, Mr Alexander McMannes, took office with his wife, Annie, as Honorary Secretary and Miss G Trevor as Treasurer. Both of these ladies held these posts for many years. The Chairperson and Secretary represented the Choral Section on the Executive Committee of the parent-Society. It was agreed that all finances from each Section would constitute a Society General Fund, but it appears that the Operatic Section's funds were already not in a healthy state. A carry-over balance at the General Meeting was showing only £2.1.11d (£2.10p). The Choral Section, starting with fifty-six members, agreed a subscription charge of 5/- (25p) for each session and section.

St Andrew's Church, Paignton was used as the location for the first Choral Section concert which was held on 30 November, 1946, with tickets priced at 5/-, 4/- and 3/- (25p, 20p and 15p). The programme included *Lauda Sion*, *Lullaby of Life* and *Our fathers to their graves have gone*. A string quartet by Mozart in D major (K155) was also played.

By the Spring of 1948, a pattern of two concerts per year had been established. On the 4 and 5 May, 1948, two parts of *Hiawatha*, with a ballet performed by the Torbay School of Music, were presented. A press-cutting reported that great difficulty was experienced in obtaining scores for both the rehearsals and the concerts and asked if anyone could loan these to the Section. This particular work appeared at quite regular intervals over the next twenty years, yet it is less common in concert programmes today. At that time, 1948, a performance of *Hiawatha* in choral form with a ballet was believed to be unique. The minutes at that date recorded a plea for members to try and recruit more tenors and basses. My reader will have read this before in earlier chapters of this book, and it will be repeated on frequent occasions throughout the rest of the century.

In June 1948, it is noted that events at the Public Hall were suddenly advertised as being performed in the Public Hall Theatre. A month later this had changed to Palace Avenue Hall Theatre and by August the title Palace Avenue Theatre appeared. This name would continue to be used throughout the rest of the century.

For the next ten years concerts given by the Choral Section were mainly located at venues in Paignton: the Palace Avenue Theatre, Palace Avenue Methodist Church and Christ Church. To set the scene regarding costs, the booking of the Torbay Orchestra and soloists for the *Elijah* concert held in the Public Hall in December, 1948, was £22 and £30 respectively. Additionally, it is also noted that the cost of hiring a rehearsal hall ranged from 15/- (75p) in the evening to 3/9d (18p) for a room in the Old Town Hall, Paignton. With tickets for the concert priced, this time, at 5/-, 3/6d and 2/6d (25p, 17½p, 12½p), a loss of £19.6.6 (£19.32½p) was sustained.

A performance by the Section in April, 1949, of varied classical items, which included two piano solos and two choral items, was poorly attended according to the 'Paignton News'. The comment was made: "With such talent one would have expected the Palace Avenue Theatre to be filled, but the poor attendance gives rise to the question are Paignton people musically inclined?" As with the matter of male voice recruitment, this theme about the lack of response from Paignton, if not Torbay, residents and visitors to more serious classical music has been repeated many times to the present day.

In May, 1950, at the Paignton & South West of England Festival of Music, Elocution, Drama and Dancing, the Choral Section qualified for the semi-finals of the Mixed Voices Choirs Class at the National Competitive Music Festival. This was to be held in Cheltenham the following February as part of the 'Festival of Britain' celebrations. Close to the date it was found that not enough members had expressed an interest in participating, so attendance was cancelled. To end the year, the Choral Section ventured into a new venue, Christ Church, Paignton, for its Christmas concert of carols and anthems.

For the 1951 'Festival of Britain' celebration, an ambitious plan, but somewhat of a gamble bearing in mind the British weather, was made to give an open-air concert of *Hiawatha* in the Oldway Mansion grounds, the former home of the Singer family, Paignton. The Paignton Male Voice and the Kingsley Choirs would be invited to join the Choral Section. Unfortunately, the idea was subsequently abandoned because of the high cost involved in hiring staging and seating.

In the article about the *Hiawatha* concert, now given on 29 November, 1951, at the Palace Avenue Theatre, the 'Paignton News' reporter noted: "allowing for the insurmountable handicap of lack of male voices, the Choral Section of Paignton ... gave a very creditable performance..." The article went on to say that Dr Barnes, the Conductor, had said: "If there are any tenors or basses left in Paignton, let them come to our aid. We need them badly."

Just after Christmas, 1951, Dr John Wray, who had been invited as Guest Conductor or accompanying organist for the Choral Section on a number of occasions, took up an appointment as Director of the London School of Music.

The difficulty of recruiting male voices was again raised at the Committee meeting in May, 1952, when concern was expressed that the performance of "big works" was in jeopardy because of this problem. In the following year the AGM decided to waive the 10/- (50p) 'down' subscription for tenors and basses in an effort to recruit more male singers. It was agreed that if a tenor or bass wished, "he could pay a weekly sum until the subscription of ten shillings was paid". So much for equal opportunities in those days! The problems in these sections of the choir continued for some time and help was sought from the Paignton Male Voice Choir and the Operatic Section to augment the Choral Section. In the 'Paignton Observer & Echo', the choir's performance of *Messiah* in December, 1953, the report stated that "the chorus singing was exceedingly good" and "well balanced". This was attributed to the fact that "for the first time the basses and tenors balanced the other voices. To those who had supported the Choir throughout its lean years, and to those members of the Paignton Male Voice Choir who have now come to its rescue, a debt of deep gratitude is due". Advertisements were already being placed in local newspapers to recruit male singers.

In January, 1954, conflict of opinions arose between the Choral and the Operatic Sections of the group Society. The Operatic Section had also sought help from the local Male Voice Choir to assist with male voices and offered free temporary membership. The Choral Section Committee had decided that those assisting from that Choir would be asked to pay the normal Section subscription fee, 10/- (50p). In the end the Executive Committee of the parent-Society overruled the Choral Section by agreeing that the extra male voices assisting should not be classed "members" and that no fee was therefore payable.

On 31 March, 1954, the Choral Section ventured into the world of light opera by performing Montague Phillips' *The Rebel Maid*. The work was chosen because it had local appeal with the story plotted around the landing of William of Orange in 1688 at Brixham. The same year, following a lengthy discussion by Committee members, the reduced choir membership led to a decision being made to give only one concert in the forthcoming season. A headline "Choral Society Lacks Male Voices" in December of that year again highlighted the situation. The article went on to say that in the work *Lauda Sion* "there is a definite need for more tenors, and with only one or two in a Society of approximately forty to fifty members it was too much to expect a perfect balance. The bass could also benefit with a little more weight". One assumes that the reference was nothing to do with physical size!

By May, 1955, it was reported that the Section had forty members regularly attending rehearsals. Later in the year in October, Dr Barnes officially resigned from the post of Conductor but said he was willing to continue until his replacement was found. At the performance of Haydn's *The Creation* in April, 1956, Dr Wray was invited back as guest conductor. Unfortunately, membership had declined and by May was down to thirty-five and twelve months later twenty-three. Dr Barnes conducted his last concert with the Choral Section on 29 November, 1956, at the Palace Avenue Methodist Church, Paignton, after exactly ten years (less two days!) as Conductor of the Section.

At a social gathering of members in February the following year Councillor Frank Martin, Chairman of the Paignton Council, made a presentation to Dr Barnes and paid tribute to his years of effort on behalf of music in Paignton. Representatives from the Fairburn Singers, for which group he was also Conductor, attended the evening. A Life Membership of the Paignton Operatic, Dramatic and Choral Society was awarded to Dr Barnes.

The AGM in 1957 confirmed the appointment of a young twenty-two year old, Mr Derek Browning, as Conductor, although Mr Denis Isles had to take over much of the year during Mr Browning's absence. One assumes that this may have been because of work commitments? Reporting on 15 May, 1957, the 'Paignton News' described the Choir Section as having been the "Cinderella" part of the Paignton Operatic, Dramatic and Choral Society because they "had often taken the back seat from the public eye". Despite this comment, the May performance which had included mime and ballet sequences by Miss Margaret Warren's School, was praised by the Chairman of Paignton Council, Councillor Martin, who said that *"Hiawatha* has been performed in Paignton before - about six years ago, I believe, but never as well as this, I was informed from several quarters".

Twelve months later Mr John Nancekevill was appointed as Conductor. The minutes show that at the Paignton Festival, an event in which the Section had competed several times since 1950, it won a First Class Certificate. The following year, however, entrance in the Festival was cancelled because of the need for additional rehearsal time for the *Judas Maccabaeus* concert in May. This particular performance marked the commemoration of the bi-centenary of the death of Handel. It was the first time the Choral Section had performed the work and some time since it had been sung in the district.

In October, 1959, a fifteen year old girl applied to join the Choir and this caused some consternation for the Committee. After a search of the rules no age restriction could be found. It was decided that all future applicants of any age should have an audition and that the Conductor should decide whether they could be admitted to the Choir.

Application to participate in the Paignton Festival was re-instated in 1960 when a First Class Certificate was again awarded. The Choral Section also took part in a concert marking the seven-hundredth Anniversary of the Paignton Parish Church. With the help of the Torquay Philharmonic Society, performances were given on Good Friday and Christmas that year. Ironically, the November concert in Christ Church included the work *Sleepers Awake* but darkness descended when all the lights fused in the Church prior to the start! Going back eighty-two years, the *Hymn of Praise* also in the programme was the first work performed by the newly-recog-nized "Paignton Choral Society". By 1961 the AGM reported that member-ship had started to go up again, although the intention to perform Brahms' *Requiem* in May had to be postponed because of insufficient rehearsal. The concert was later cancelled altogether. At the Meeting mentioned earlier, Mr Nancekevill stated that he was prepared to continue as Conductor only if the Choral Section changed its constitution in order to come under the Devon Education Authority and be affiliated to the Arts Council. The result of this and other matters was that the Choir faced unsettling issues for the next couple of years. A request to change the constitution was rejected by the Executive Committee of the parent-Society. A vote of confidence at an Extra-ordinary meeting was requested by the Chairperson, Mr Forrester, and the meeting was asked to decide whether Mr Nancekevill should continue as Conductor. A decision was taken to appoint a replacement and in July, 1961, Mr William Humpherson was offered the position.

The Choral Section in May, 1962, again achieved success with a First Class Certificate at the Paignton & South West Festival when *Jesu, joy of man's desiring* was performed. On 30 August, 1962, the 'Paignton Observer & Echo', started in 1889, and claiming to be the only independent newspaper in Paignton, closed following a merger with the 'Paignton News'. The latter now became the only remaining 'town' paper for important advertising and publicity, although the loss of the 'Observer' meant that a helpful means of reviewing local events was lost.

To perform Haydn's *The Seasons* in May, 1963, described by the 'Paignton News' as a "forgotten work", difficult decisions were faced requiring an Extra-ordinary meeting to be held by the Choral Section. Finances and membership had reached a low ebb. The Chairperson threatened to resign and asked for a vote of confidence which was unanimously given. Despite these problems, the concerts went ahead and even the Secretary himself was willing to lend £10 towards the expenses if money was not forthcoming. Another First Class Certificate was awarded to the Choir at the Paignton Festival in 1963. At Christmas that year, *Messiah* was performed in Christ Church. With the help of the Torquay Philharmonic and the Tor Choral Society (believed to include many members of the choir at All Saints Church, Torquay), a force of one hundred voices was obtained. A footnote in the 'Paignton News' noted that Mr Humpherson, the Conductor, had promised "to those who have suffered, before, this time the Church (Christ Church) will be heated".

A deficit of £102 showed in the Choral Section's accounts in January, 1964, causing great concern to the Committee. Through jumble sales and other events it was hoped that the financial situation would be improved and each member was asked to raise a sum of £1 individually or in groups. It was also agreed that the AGM would take place in March instead of June in order to fit in with the end of the financial year. At this meeting the longest-serving Chairperson of the Choral Section, Mr Forrester, stood down after eleven years in office. With finances in such a serious state grant-aid was sought from the National Federation of Musical Societies for the 1964/5 season. A sum of £29 was eventually awarded by the Arts Council towards any concert losses.

The regular use of the Palace Avenue Methodist and Christ Churches for concerts was broken in May, 1964 when Britten's *St Nicolas*, believed to be the first performance of the work in the Torbay area, was presented at St Paul's Church, Preston, Paignton. Girls from Stover School, Newton Abbot, joined the Choir for the semi-chorus parts.

The award of a Cup was again made to the Choral Section at the 1965 South West of England Festival. In December of that year Mr Humpherson resigned from the post of Conductor because he was moving to Salisbury. Mr Bruce Ferris, Music Teacher at Newton Abbot Grammar School, was appointed and had to face the problem as to whether to give a concert the following Spring. He decided, with the Committee's approval, to perform *St John's Passion* in October with the Torquay Philharmonic. However, it was reported at the AGM in 1966 that membership had dropped to twenty-seven members. As the number of Torquay Philharmonic players was also low, a Christmas concert was planned instead. In the meantime a partnership had been built up with St John's Church Choir, the Strand, Torquay, to swell singing numbers.

The Choral Society's affiliation to the Paignton Operatic, Dramatic and Choral Society was causing increasing frustration, and this situation would not come to a head until 1982. An example of this happened in Spring, 1966, when the Conductor asked for an honorarium of £30 which included his travel costs to and from his home in Kingsteignton, Newton Abbot, for rehearsals. The Executive Committee rejected this and delicate re-negotiations had to take place with Mr Ferris by the Choral Section Committee.

In the summer, after five months as Conductor, Mr Ferris stood down owing to other commitments. Mr Archibald Marcom took over from the September of that year. At the first Committee meeting Mr Forrester returned to the Chair and was again to remain for a further four years, adding to his record as previously having been the longest serving Chairman of the Society and Section. The Committee agreed later in 1967 (in recognition of this dedication to the Choir) that he should be made Life Member.

The partnership mentioned earlier with St John's Church resulted in the performance of Schubert's *Mass* at their Church in November, 1966, and again on All Saints Day, in January, 1967. The Church Choir reciprocated by joining the Choral Section's performance of Haydn's *The Creation* at Christ Church three months later in April. It was hoped that Bach's *Christmas Oratorio* could have been performed in December, but this had to be postponed because of lack of rehearsals and the change of Conductor. The 1967/8 season was also the twenty-first anniversary of the Choral Section's re-formation after the Second World War and a celebratory dinner was held at the Corbyn Head Hotel, Torquay. Nowadays one hears of supporters' clubs particularly in sport, but on a Tuesday and Wednesday in November, a special event for Vice-Presidents and supporters of the Paignton Operatic, Dramatic and Choral Society entitled "Further Happening" was presented in the Palace Avenue Theatre. All three Sections contributed to the two evenings' entertainment when the Choral section sang *The Blue Danube*, *Invitation to the Dance*, *the Holy Child* and *Gloria in Excelsis Deo*.

In June, 1967, an important new venue described as a multi-purpose building which included a theatre, exhibition and dancing facilities opened. The Festival Theatre was designed by Cyril Thurley with first early estimates for its construction put at £55,000, but by the time it had opened this had risen to £400,000. The theatre had a proscenium of 40ft (just over 12m) and could seat an audience of fourteen hundred and seventy-four with removable seating which could be stored under the stage when required. This proved to be a major downfall in the design. The first production to appear was the 'Black and White Minstrels Show' which was subsequently repeated several times in following years. Within weeks of the Theatre's opening complaints were being received that vision of the stage was difficult in many of the seat positions. Some members of the Council attended a performance to see for themselves. Subsequently a sum of £3,500 was approved for timber raking in the auditorium: before this the audience had been on a flat floor space, but by October, 1967, steel flooring was approved, at a cost of £7,500. By December the work had been completed for the Christmas performance of 'Sleeping Beauty on Ice'. However, despite the seating improvements, visibility in the back rows was still presenting a problem and bookings in this section had to be withdrawn from sale by the Box Office at the Theatre. The Festival Theatre, as will be seen in the coming pages, was to be used by the Choral Section for many performances, particularly its Christmas concerts and there were to be appearances with several famous orchestras.

In May, 1968, the 'Paignton News' praised the celebration concert of *Hiawatha* with a ballet provided by the Gillian Longman School of Dancing. The comment was made that the Choral Section had contributed "a lot to music in Paignton over the years keeping its flag flying against odds". The value of other choirs joining forces for big works yet retaining their individual identities was encouraged. Further praise for the *Hiawatha* performance came at the AGM in 1968, when it was stated that there had been a full house at the Palace Avenue Theatre with "many being turned away" and also membership had increased to thirty-three.

A performance of Edward German's *Merrie England*, combining ballet and choral music, was presented in April, 1969. On this occasion the Pamela de Waal School was used for the dancing sequences. A reporter from the 'Paignton News' stated that "the four soloists always had a smile on their faces and the conductor, Mr Archibald Marcom, was prone to winking at the audience. This sort of thing, though trivial, always helps break the ice with the audience". Choir membership by this time had risen by fourteen to forty-seven. For the Good Friday concert in 1970 an ambitious idea was considered to use the Festival Theatre on the Esplanade in Paignton. Bearing in mind the seating capacity of over fourteen hundred the Choral Section was taking a large gamble. It was hoped to invite the Brixham Male Voice Choir, Torbay Singers and Brixham Crusaders to join the concert. However, permission to book the Theatre was refused by the Society Executive Committee, as it had overall responsibility for the finances of each Section. The Choral Section Committee was upset again by a decision which was seen as a further interference from the parent-body in the running of the Section. As a result of this, plan B was put into operation to perform another 'first' for the Choir, *Tom Jones*. As in the early stages of this chapter, it is interesting to note how prices had changed from the 1948 figures quoted and those later in this chapter in the 80's and 90's. To perform *Tom Jones* at the Palace Avenue Theatre, £250 was estimated as the total cost of the performance. Tickets in various parts of the Hall were priced at 10/6d (52½p), 7/6d (37½p) and 5/- (25p) with programmes selling at 1/- (5p) each. A loss of £98 was reported to the Committee following the concert.

For the 1970/71 season the Catholic Hall, Cecil Road, Paignton, was being used for rehearsals. By Spring, 1971, the Committee had suggested that a choral version of *Carmen* might be performed at the Palace Avenue Theatre. However, the AGM recommended that the 1970 decision to perform a combined choir concert at the Festival Theatre should be revived. It was decided to present Handel's *Messiah*. A Committee member offered a £150 loan to assist costs if needed, although the National Federation of Music Societies did award a grant towards the concert expenses which were estimated at £575 for use of the Theatre. Other singers were invited to join the Section and in the end the choir had increased to one hundred and nine in number. (A newspaper article of the time reported this to be one hundred and twenty, but journalists and even publicity officers are prone to exaggerate at times!) The 'Paignton News' 'Backstage' reporter described the *Messiah* as a "brave" performance by the Conductor, Mr Marcom, who used "a lot of Handel's original score rather than the 'easier edited' versions". The final audience numbers attending cannot be traced, but the Choral Section Committee minutes state that "many were turned away owing to no seats being available". Seven hundred and fifty programmes were sold with an income from ticket sales of £659.50 – decimalization had come into being by that time – and an overall profit of £180 had been made.

It was hoped that for the 1971/2 season continued use of the Catholic Hall might be possible. This was not the case, and the Section moved to Winner Street Baptist Church for the season. As 1971 marked the twenty-fifth anniversary of the Association, a return to the Festival Theatre for the Choral Section was decided. This time *Elijah* was suggested with the Choir being joined by the London Capriol Orchestra for accompaniment, and invitations, again, extended to other choirs. The use of this Orchestra was subsequently rejected when high costs became apparent and negotiations took place for the Band of HM Royal Marines to take part. This, however, also fell through because of the intervention of the Musicians' Union, which prevented the Band from playing. A return to the original idea to engage the Capriol Orchestra was resurrected. The costs had now increased to £960 for the performance and even though it was minuted that a thousand people attended, a heavy loss was incurred. In addition to this concert the Choral Section held its Silver Jubilee Anniversary Dinner on 23 March, 1972, attended by seventy-two members and friends. At the AGM the following month members were informed that the membership now stood at seventy-eight. At the same meeting Mr Forrester was presented with a NODA (National Operatic and Dramatic Association) medal for twenty-five years' service in operatic and choral work. Mrs McMannes stood down as Honorary Secretary of the Choral Section, a post which she had occupied since the first meeting after the Second World War, 26 years before.

The concert dress to be worn by the ladies was considered by the Committee in May, 1972, with a decision reached that they should wear long black skirts and white blouses. Previously skirts had been knee length – a potential embarrassment for front row ladies on a stage when the audience were at a much lower level. A spokesperson was appointed to answer "all the queries that would undoubtedly come from the ladies"!

A further change in the 1972/3 season took place when the Choir moved to Oldway Primary School, Higher Polsham Road, Paignton for rehearsals. Another problem for the Choral Section, and in fact all societies and businesses – Value Added Tax (VAT) – reared its head when planning was taking place for the use of the Festival Theatre for a third time in April, 1973, for Bach's *St Matthew Passion*. This immediately raised the cost of hiring the Theatre and even increased the fee for the bass soloist. For the first time the girls from Marist Convent School, Paignton, helped in the double chorus parts in the work. The strain of putting on these concerts at the Festival Theatre was the reason given by Mr Marcom when he resigned as Conductor in Summer 1973. He stated that he did not wish to jeopardize the success of any future concerts given by the Section. Mr Fred Duerden was subsequently appointed to replace Mr Marcom. The Committee was also concerned, yet again, as a loss resulted from the *St Matthew Passion* concert.

Visits by the Chairperson in 1973 to decide where the *Messiah* perform-ance might be presented in that year, revealed that only three church venues could be used: St Andrew's, St Paul's or Christ Church. In the end, Christ Church was selected. Twelve pupils were used from Marist Convent School for the second time and were invited to become junior members of the Choral Section at 50p each. Previously junior members had been turned away because of their age. This link with the School also seems to have been a ploy to gain the services of the Convent's music teacher as Deputy Conductor.

In February, 1974, lighting at rehearsals posed a problem because of the miners' strike which might restrict power supplies in the Paignton area at times. It was felt that if this happened, insufficient rehearsals might affect the standard of singing. It was suggested that some rehearsals might be moved to Saturday and Sunday afternoons to gain the advantage of natural daylight. It is not known whether things came to a point where this measure had to be put into effect. A new musical field was explored for the May concert when it was decided to perform 'An Evening of Gilbert & Sullivan' in concert form. Unfortunately, it was later discovered after rehearsals had started that a G&S performance was to be given by a professional touring group which would be at the Festival Theatre, Paignton, the week prior to the Choral Section's concert. Ironically a Theatre advertisement in the local newspaper showed both forthcoming events in the same allocated space. The Choral Society concert made a loss which it was felt was because audiences had 'had their fill' of the duo's music! The concert was attended by a group of fifty-seven members of a visiting choir to the area from Hameln, Germany, with which Torbay is twinned. The Section members gave the German visitors coffee and biscuits after the performance and an invitation was extended by them for the Choral Section to visit Germany at some time in the future for a concert.

The Christmas concert held in the Festival Theatre in December, 1974, was given a new image with the title 'Sing Noel'. This successful name, championed by the Chairperson at the time, Mike Griffiths, was used on-and-off for advertising the Choral Section's Christmas concerts for the next sixteen years. For the first time a Production Sub-Committee was formed to manage and give the seasonal concert a more professional presentation. The 'Sing Noel' concert was accompanied by the Paignton Citadel Salvation Army Band, conducted by Mr Harold Hoar, who was to become the Choral Section's conductor later from 1982 to 1986. At the Christmas concert two Section members, Grace Reed and Alice Down, who had a record of twenty-five and thirty-five years respectively of singing with the Section, received medals from the Paignton Operatic,

Dramatic and Choral Society in recognition of this service. (Quite how this was calculated for Alice Down is not quite clear, as the Choral Section had only existed for twenty-six years after the War, but it is assumed that the additional calculated nine years service was either with the Operatic Section during the war or with the Choral Society pre-war.)

In the Summer of 1975 the Chairperson reported that, although there had been rumblings for the Choral Section to become an independent choir, the suggestion had been dropped. At that stage it was felt that the security of belonging to a collective Society was important and that separation would have constitutional problems. At the AGM the subscription was agreed at £2.50 for membership of one Section, £4 for two Sections and £5 for three. In preparation for the May Brahms' *Requiem* performance, the choir attended additional rehearsals during the week so that voice sections could be given individual attention.

In May, 1976, the 'Paignton News' was renamed 'Torbay News' with "more pages", and it would be a "handier size" it was claimed, thus reflecting the wider area of reporting and news.

By late 1977, the choir had continued to grow, but there was an imbalance of voices due to the "ever increasing" number of sopranos. Tactful methods of asking certain ladies to withdraw from the Christmas concert as "their failing powers were becoming more apparent" were considered by the Committee and Conductor. Help from two other members of the Choir was sought to assist the Conductor in auditioning new members when necessary. A shortage of male voices again led to advertising, letters being sent to other choirs, and choir members were asked to see if they had friends who might be interested in choral work. Further problems were aired when the Committee reviewed the Christmas 'Sing Noel' concert held that year. It appeared that the unreserved seating policy adopted by the Choir at the Festival Theatre meant that crowds assembled at the entrances. There was then a free-for-all rush to gain seats when the doors opened and people were leaving coats on seats to reserve them for their friends. This had led to frayed tempers amongst other members of the audience and even abuse of Theatre staff who, in turn, complained to the Choral Section. It was decided that in future the unreserved policy might have to be abandoned.

The AGM in 1978 debated a number of issues including the format of the Christmas concerts and the possibility of performing a work such as *Elijah* at some time in the coming season. Mr Duerden, Conductor at the time, advised that this was not possible because, despite being a large choir, there was still a lack of male singers. The Chairperson at the next Committee meeting produced a number of ideas and ways in which the prestige of the choir could be built up. He suggested that concerts might in future include big works with national or international soloists and famous orchestras. This led to a lively debate for some time at the meeting. The lengthy minutes recorded that some comments from the Chairperson were finally greeted with a "stunned silence" – or maybe it was just the lateness of the hour (10.45pm)! Many of the issues were discussed by the Committee at various stages in future years.

The 'Sing Noel' concert at the Festival Theatre was planned for the 9 December, but this had to be moved back because on that date the Royal Philharmonic Orchestra was presenting a concert which included Holst's *Planet Suite*. The ladies section in the choir was invited to sing and thirty-six members (twelve from each section of first and second sopranos and altos) took part in the work. It is believed that the invitation came as a result of discussions by the Committee with the Torbay Borough Entertainments Officer concerning the role the choir might take in the musical world of Torbay. The selection of which lady singers might be used opened a 'whole can of worms' to such an extent that the recruitment might have had to go outside the Choral Section to the Operatic Section or even other choirs. As a first step it was decided that all lady members should be auditioned for the Holst Performance, but it was felt that this would also provide an opportunity to "regrade some of the sopranos". By November, 1978, many of the ladies' voices had been reviewed. It was discovered that some first sopranos had wrongly classified themselves previously and "should not be in the society at all". One lady, whose poor voice quality was often heard above others and which had been remarked upon, stoutly refused to be budged from her seat in the first sopranos. After an exchange of correspondence she was asked to appear before the Committee to explain her refusal to move. When eventually the Chairperson interviewed her, she robustly questioned the competence of any Committee members to judge the ability of her singing and that she had been assured by persons holding higher qualifications that her voice was "as good as ever". Further, she claimed that as she read music and had sung soprano for forty years she would be unable to sing alto. A contradiction in terms? With no final compromise reached she returned to her section. The Committee hoped that the issue might resolve itself in some way. By June the following year the remaining choir members had nearly all been, or would be, auditioned as had new potential members some of whom were rejected from membership of the choir.

The Choral Section concert was put back to the 16 December and the reserved seat policy was maintained although, in the light of past experience, the opinion of the Committee was somewhat divided on the subject. A Producer, Mr John Richardson, was appointed at a fee of £60 to make the concert arrangements. Prior to the concert the important issue as to whether the ladies should tuck their blouses inside their skirt waistbands or wear them outside in a "junior miss" style was debated. This appears to have been just as controversial an issue as reserved seats. The local newspaper reported that the Christmas concert was broadcast by the BBC the night before the concert happened but, in fact, it was recorded beforehand for a 15 December radio broadcast.

The result of on-going discussions over the previous years with Paul Clifford, Borough Entertainments Officer mentioned earlier, was that the Choral Section received further invitations to take part in some prestigious concerts. The first was with the Bournemouth Symphony Orchestra in November, 1979, and the second the following Christmas with the Band of the Life Guards who were accompanied by the Trumpeters of the Household Cavalry. For the former a Choirmaster was appointed to assist the Conductor in rehearsals of the Brahms' *German Requiem*. Mr Hoar, mentioned earlier in 1974 when he was conducting the Paignton Citadel Salvation Army Band, was appointed to this position. Although the Brahms performance, conducted by Norman Del Mar of the BSO was a success (the 'Herald Express' used headlines "Quite glorious choral vocalism") the concert was poorly attended. As a consequence the Borough Entertainments Officer needed to reimburse the choir for the cost of staging and music. He also offered to meet some of the finances for an afternoon and evening performance of the now traditional 'Sing Noel' in the Festival Theatre on 23 December. This date was, however, re-negotiated to an earlier date in December and reduced to an evening performance only.

It is unclear from the records in the Society's possession whether the Paignton Operatic, Dramatic and Choral Society raised any objections, but it is noted that both in the minutes and in printed publicity, a change of title for the Choral Section suddenly took place at the end of the 70's. The full title shown earlier, which had always appeared in documents, suddenly changed to 'Paignton Choral Society', thus giving the Section an individual identity. It was acknowledged in the programme for a little time further that it was still a Section of the corporate body but this was to change two years later.

In March, 1980, the Festival Theatre was used yet again, when the Bristol Sinfonia joined the choir for a performance of Handel's *Messiah*. The difficulty of getting "bums on seats" was highlighted in the 'Herald Express' article headlined "Half-filled hall for £3000 Messiah".

Later that year an old stamping ground, the Palace Avenue Theatre used by the Society for so many years before the two World Wars, was under threat of closure. The Council, hard pushed for cash, indicated that it was prepared to offer a ninety-nine year lease for a commercial or community development of the Theatre or demolish it. Considerable space was devoted in Chapters 1 and 2 of this book to examine the debate which took place as the Theatre had gradually outlived its original usefulness and required up-dating. Although the Theatre had not been used for many years, the Society worried about this and organized a petition. This, with many other petitions from the public, was handed to the Mayor on 17 November, 1980, – the day the Council was to make a decision regarding the Theatre's fate. After two referrals back to the Recreation Committee in February, 1981, the Council recommended that the Theatre should remain as a community resource.

In 1980, the Society included a number of seasonal items in its programme of 'Sing Noel' at the Festival Theatre in December and was accompanied by the Band of the Life Guards. Also during 1980 the Devon Education Authority invited the Society to participate in a performance of Verdi's *Requiem* at Exeter Cathedral. A "significant proportion" of the choir attended rehearsals and took part in the performance in May, 1981. The same month, in contrast to the size of the Cathedral, the Paignton Parish Church, with a seating capacity of six hundred, was almost full for the Society's presentation of music by Haydn and Vivaldi. It is interesting to note that, despite the fact that the Society had originated in Paignton one hundred and ten years earlier and performed nearly always in that town, the Parish Church was used only twice for a concert and this was the first occasion. The Church, with its chancel wooden screen, did present problems. The choir was hidden if the Church choir stalls were used, and space for audience was lost if the choir came out in rows in front of the screen.

In November, 1981, the Torbay Youth Orchestra joined the Society for a 'Music to Remember' evening with a wide range and varied programme of operatic, classical and negro spirituals and other music. Because of increasing hire costs and its experience in failing to attract crowds to the Festival Theatre, the Choral Society returned to the Palace Avenue Theatre for the Christmas 'Sing Noel' in December. The Torbay Brass Band was invited to accompany the Society in parts of the programme.

At an historic AGM of the Society on 1 February, 1982, members were informed that the Paignton Operatic, Dramatic and Choral Society Executive had approved a split of the Sections into the 'Paignton Operatic and Dramatic Society', and the 'Paignton Choral Society'. The effective date was 1 June, 1982. The Headquarters building (close to the Paignton Rugby ground and since demolished) used by the old Society, for which there had been a Building fund for many years, was relinquished by the Choral Section because of its unsuitability for use by the choir. It is worth adding that frustration had been experienced by the Choral Section Committee that permission had to be sought from the parent-executive before a programme could be announced. On occasions some concerts were refused on the grounds of lack of funds, and profits for more successful events were creamed off into the main group's coffers. As mentioned earlier, the title of Paignton Choral Society was already being used for publicity, paving the way for this eventual break. The split from the main Society required the preparation of new documents including the constitution and a set of rules. It was also reported at the AGM that Norman Del Mar had been invited to become the first President of the newly formed Society, a post which he subsequently accepted. This sixty-two year old conductor, mentioned previously when he conducted the Bournemouth Symphony Orchestra in 1979 with the Society, regularly appeared at the BBC Promenade Concerts including three "Last Nights". In the 1960's he had been Conductor of the BBC Scottish Orchestra and had received a CBE in recognition of his general service to the world of music.

Later in 1982 the Minutes of the Society noted that for the previous few years there had been no orchestral accompaniment for works performed by the Society except at Christmas Carol events. Lack of sponsors and funds to pay the expenses appeared to have been the problem.

By 1983 an experiment to perform the same work, in this case *Elijah* on two successive dates at different venues, was ventured. Later reviews of the plan showed that audiences at both concerts had been disappointingly small, probably because of the close proximity of the two churches used – St Paul's Church and Christ Church, Paignton. This provoked considerable discussion at the 1984 AGM. It was also recorded that membership was on the increase, with nearly eighty members compared to the previous year when it was seventy. Since the Society had appointed its first President, Mr Del Mar, and its split from the original joint association, this gentleman had moved to London. The Committee felt that the need to find a local personality was important and Mr Del Mar agreed to stand down from the position.

At the first meeting after the AGM in that year the first 'rumblings' by a member, Alan Hawkins, were made about the Society becoming a registered charity. This, in turn, could incorporate covenanting which would assist the Society through tax refunds. It must be said, at this stage, steps to register the Society received a cool reception from the majority of the Committee, but the 'rumblings' grew louder in successive years as we will read later. The question of an orchestra regularly accompanying concerts was also raised again later in the year. It was suggested that it might be formed from local music teachers and that the Senior Area Music Tutor for Devon County Council, Mr Melvyn Batten, should be approached. At this stage, Mr Batten's response to the Committee was that this was not possible. However, this idea later became a reality.

A problem not experienced before arose in the planning of the Christmas 1985 'Sing Noel' concert. The inclusion of a school choir did not materialize because of an industrial dispute involving one of the teachers' unions. Further frustrations were encountered when an ambitious plan to perform the *Verdi Requiem* in May, 1986 had to be cancelled because of that recurring problem, lack of male singers. Despite an advertisement in the local newspaper for additional men, no response was forthcoming.

The following May the last concert by the Conductor, Mr Hoar, was held at another venue not previously used. It was felt that concerts in Torquay had a better following of audiences than Paignton and, therefore, Central Church in Torquay was hired. It may be of interest to note here that in 1971, as a result of discussions by the Church Councils of three nineteenth century Torquay Methodist churches in Union Street, one in Market Street and the Belgrave at Torre were all in need of repairs. It was decided to sell the two former buildings and demolish the church on the latter site in order to erect a new modern building. A year later the plans were drawn up for the new church to be known as a United Reformed Church and in 1975 the foundation stone was laid. This modern multi-use venue with its three dominant external crosses above the main entrance, has inside an elongated octagonal shape with an area for congregation, choir and an altar. An adjoining hall complete with a stage is separated, if required, by a sliding partitioned screen from the main part of the church. The Central Church opened the following year for services and was to be, and still is, the 'home' for concerts by the Society on many occasions.

At the AGM in June, 1986, because of small audiences and resulting low ticket sales, the members decided to perform only two concerts in the coming season. It was at this stage that there was a change of Director of Music with Mr Melvyn Batten being appointed from September, 1986. An attempt at the AGM to move the Society towards charity status was made but the motion was defeated mainly because the accounting procedures needed to be more formally recorded and audited. The meeting also expressed and placed on record its appreciation to Mrs Margaret Penfold, the current accompanist, who had been a member of the choir for thirty years.

After taking up the post, Mr Batten changed the content of the planned November, 1986, programme to a performance of *St Nicolas* and *Zadok the Priest*. It was at this concert that the Festival Orchestra made its first appearance. Because of Mr Batten's position as a Senior Area Music Tutor, he was able to bring together local music teachers and tutors to form this ad hoc group, the formation of which had been suggested by the Choral Society Committee a couple of years earlier. The Orchestra is still used by the South Devon Choir, as it is now known today, and the instrumentalists now come from a wide area in the county and outside with a regular use of some students at music colleges or universities. For the sub-chorus in *St Nicolas,* Torquay Girls' Grammar School provided singers for the children's parts. The following month, the usual 'Sing Noel' concert at the Festival Theatre included three school choirs (Mr Batten was using his contacts), hand-bell ringers and a chamber orchestra. However, the event came in for criticism from one source because the National Anthem was omitted. How things have changed since, with "God save the Queen" rarely played at the start or the end of performances unless, of course, royalty is actually present. The South Devon Choir is still awaiting that honour!

At the first Committee meeting in February, 1987, after the concerts which were reported as successes, membership was showing a steady increase back up to the figures of the early eighties. Mr Batten expressed the hope that eventually the choir would have one hundred and fifty members with an ideal split of fifty-five sopranos, thirty-three altos, twenty-five tenors and thirty-five basses (someone obviously could not add up unless the Minute Secretary incorrectly recorded the figures)! Two months later the death in April of Margaret Penfold, the Society's previous accompanist mentioned earlier, was recorded. By this time Sue Merry-weather, a teacher and private music tutor, had taken up the post of accompanist and continued in that appointment to the end of the century.

By the AGM, 1987, records show that warning bells were being sounded about the finances of the Society and concert costs. The Conductor, Mr Batten, responded by saying that he had laid down conditions when he had accepted the appointment. He stated "that money must not dictate the performance and programme of the Society. It is up to its members to raise the finance to support its music programmme" and that more performances during the year were necessary. He wanted these so that new singers would be encouraged to join and bring in regular audiences.

For the first time on 18 April, 1988, the full Society (as far as can be traced from the records) performed outside the immediate area. In the second half of a concert in the Plymouth Guidlhall by the Devon Schools' Symphonic Wind Band for which Mr Batten was the Conductor, the Society with the Plymouth Philharmonic Choir sang in a 'Last Night of the Proms' style programme. With much waving of flags, all the usual favourites including *Rule Britannia* and *Jerusalem* were sung. The following day at the Society's Committee meeting, an idea was put forward by Stephen Auger, Conductor of the North Devon Choral Society and Mr Batten's opposite number in North Devon as Area Music Tutor, that the two Choirs should combine for a concert in the north and south of Devon. A plan for a 1989 performance of works by Berlioz and Kodaly seemed a good opportunity to put this in place.

To return to the financial problems mentioned earlier: a successful application to South West Arts produced a £600 grant and Torbay Council agreed to underwrite the loss on the *Dream of Gerontius* performed in June, 1988. Unfortunately, the £500 offered was later cut by half because the Council considered the Society was being too ambitious. The Treasurer's report at the AGM for the year ending 31 May, five days after the concert, indicated a £1,780 deficiency. A request for a loan from the Society's bankers was refused. Through the connections of the Society's Honorary Auditor the Society's account was transferred to a more sympathetic bank which was prepared to underwrite the loss until the start of the new season when subscriptions came in. In the meantime urgent attempts were made to find sponsors. The June AGM also involved another major step in the Society's life. In keeping with the changes at South West Arts for grant-aid and the wider residential area from which members now came, a change of the Society's name to the 'Paignton & South Devon Choral Society' was recommended to the membership by the Committee and to move it forward to registered charity status. Formal approval for these changes was put to the members at the AGM and was unanimously approved. The change of title and several minor amendments to the Society's rules were subsequently submitted to the Charity Commissioners for approval and were accepted. The added bonus of charity status was that the Covenant Scheme, since named Gift-aid, entitled the Society to recover through the Inland Revenue a percentage of the subscription charge by any member who was paying tax.

In the past, in 1975, an industrial dispute with the miners had affected choir rehearsals because of lighting and heating problems. Then in 1985 a teachers' union work-to-rule prevented a school choir from taking part in a Christmas concert that year. Now, in September, 1988, another dispute reared its head: plans to put the covenanting scheme into practice as the Society reached the point of becoming a registered charity were thwarted by a postal strike.

At the start of this season a replacement piano was purchased and plans were put in place for the first trip abroad for the Society with the North Devon Choral Society. On the 29 November, with other guest choirs, the Society sang outside the area again, this time in the grandeur of Exeter Cathedral. A 'Candlelight Carolcade' was performed for the National Children's Home charity and included TV personalities Leslie Crowther, comedian, and Angela Rippon, television presenter, as compères. The Society was also invited to be guest choir, accompanied by the Torquay

Salvation Army Band, for the first time at the Civic Carol Concert in December at the (then named) English Riviera Centre.

By the Summer of 1989 finances featured again as a problem, as well as male membership of the choir. Grants from South West Arts had ceased because of government cut-backs in their funding, as did the Council grant. As a method of raising finance for the Society a '100 Club' was started. Members were invited to pay a set amount each month with a monthly draw of three prizes. The latter was approximately fifty per cent of the money collected with the remainder allocated to Society funds. The club is still running today and provides a useful regular income. Despite the concern caused by funds, morale in the choir was kept high with the anticipation of the visit to the Quimper Festival in Brittany, France, and the performances in Central Church of the *Te Deum* by Berlioz and *Te Deum* by Kodaly on 10 June with the North Devon Choral Society, and the return visit to Ilfracombe the following day performing in the town's main church.

Two months later a total of eighty-seven singers from the Society with their North Devon counterpart arrived in France to sing at Saint-Corentin Cathedral as part of the 11th 'Semaines Musicales de Quimper' on 17 August, 1989. All members and their family or friends met their own costs, but the Festival Orchestra (renamed on this occasion as the 'West of England Symphony Orchestra') received a £2,000 grant from the Quimper Festival organizers towards their expenses. The event was greatly enjoyed by all even though, for some people, a plague of mosquitoes, the spartan accommodation including iron bedsteads and communal toilets was rather a culture shock! The relationships that were built up, especially at the late night party held after the concert, bonded the choirs in a different way from the two brief hours spent at normal rehearsals at home in Devon. This encouraged the Paignton & South Devon Choral Society Conductor to suggest that a 'Three Choirs Festival' might be held between his own Society, the North Devon Choral Society and the Plymouth Philharmonic Choir with concerts every two years being held at different venues. Although the Festival idea did not come to fruition for many years, the societies mentioned joined the Paignton Society at various concerts before the end of the century. A further development to change the image of the Society took place with the use of a new logo on its headed notepaper and for general publicity. New folders were also purchased to hold singers' music at concerts to provide the choir with some visual uniformity.

At a Committee Meeting in November, 1989, news was received that the Society had again been invited to participate in the Quimper Music Festival. For this occasion the grant from the Festival Committee would not cover the total cost of the orchestra so some of this would have to be shared by the members of the societies travelling to France. Early in 1990 it was also learned that Torbay's twinned town in Holland, Hellevoetsluis, would be hosting a ladies' choir and that they would link up with the Society for a concert at Central Church in May, 1991.

On 29 April, 1990, as part of the Golden Jubilee of the Torbay and South-West of England Festival of Dance, Drama, Music and Verse, the Society performed an extract of the *Messiah* at the Festival Theatre, Paignton. In the Summer of that year another 'first' venue for a choir concert was used when the English Riviera Centre was booked with its auditorium seating twelve hundred. The choir had sung in the Centre previously for two Civic Carol concerts. Additional singers from the Devon County Choir were recruited to augment the Society's own members for this work new to the Society, Vaughan Williams' *A Sea Symphony*. Despite good numbers attending, a deficit of £3,500 resulted.

At the AGM held later in the year, a Vice Presidency scheme was set up. It is worth recording that at this stage subscriptions had now increased to £40 per season and £50 for the new Vice Presidents.

During the late Spring and early Summer months, seventy-one members and their friends indicated that they would be travelling to Quimper. This time better accommodation in a boarding school was promised. A grant of £2,750 was secured, again for orchestral expenses. With the North Devon Choral Society a performance of Beethoven's *Missa Solemnis* was given in the Cathedral on Friday, 10 August and Bach's *Mass in C* at the Eglise St Mathieu on Sunday, 12 August. The Friday concert commenced fifteen minutes late when the main fuses on the organ blew. An electrician had to be found in a hurry to carry out repairs amidst a slow hand-clap from the packed audience! The Sunday concert experienced a different type of problem when the English choirs almost refused to sing because of the attitude of the German conductor whose choir also joined the Festival. He was reputed to be a Bach specialist and perfectionist and treated all singers accordingly, including his own choir, with strict musical discipline. Fortunately, relationships amongst all members of all the choirs remained cordial and another post-concert celebration lasted into the very early hours of the following morning.

Earlier in 1990, the Torbay Singers were contacted with the intention to develop a closer link between the two Societies' singers and Conductors. After a meeting attended by some Officers from both Committees and the two Conductors, it was agreed to exchange information about dates of concerts, works to be performed and to make insertions of forthcoming events in each other's concert programmes. The setting up of a local music-diary to co-ordinate concerts of societies in the area was also suggested. (It took over eight years for this to take effect.) As a result of this meeting, a group from the Paignton Choral Society joined the Torbay Singers on 15 December to perform Bach's *Christmas Oratorio* at St Mary the Virgin Church, St Marychurch, Torquay. Further attempts to gain greater publicity for the Paignton Society were made when the Deputy Editor of the 'Herald Express', Mike Thompson, was invited to a Committee meeting in late 1990.

In March, 1991, another new location was used for the performance of Vivaldi's *Gloria*. To fit a large choir into the fixed choir pews in many churches presented considerable problems. Thus St Luke's Church, Shedden Hill, Torquay, became the concert venue this time. This difficulty of space recurred on a number of occasions in the future and was an issue that the Committee very often had to consider when deciding where to hold concerts. For the first time the Society also became the sponsor for someone else when the Devon Wind Band was invited to play in April, 1991, at Central Church. This brought in a useful profit of £500.

On 11 May, 1991, approximately sixty members of the Dutch Ladies' Choir from Hellevoetsluis, some of whom were hosted by choir members, performed a varied concert with the Paignton Choral Society at Central Church. Following this it was hoped that a return visit might be made to sing the *Messiah* in Holland. This was warmly welcomed by the Halvoets Dameskoor Choir.

By the Summer months some ideas were put into effect for fund raising. Following warnings by the Society's Treasurer in January that the accounts were precariously low, a brain-storming session by the Committee produced possible ways of remedying the situation. By the Summer months members of the choir were seen walking around clutching Smartie tubes. Having eaten all the sweets, even if singers claimed they were on a diet, they were invited to replace the contents with 20p pieces with every full tube raising about £13 for Choir funds. A Hymn Marathon in June, 1991, was organized at the Palace Avenue Methodist Church, Paignton – an old haunt of the choir but now modernized – and proceeds were split between the Church and the Society. The combination of Smartie tubes and hymns realized just over £860 for Society funds. Finally, further financial aid came when the Plymouth & South Devon Co-operative Society agreed to sponsor the choir, subject to certain conditions, for £1,000 to the end of 1991.

Despite the financial problems, the very ambitious performance, on a large scale, of the Verdi *Requiem* was given at the Festival Theatre in June. There were one hundred and seventy in the choir including the guest singers. It is believed that for the first time in the Society's history a Sunday performance was arranged and this drew a large audience.

By January, 1992, the 1991/2 season was helped by a grant of £350 received from South West Arts. Torbay Council had allocated £500 as indemnity against losses. It may be recalled that earlier in June, 1988, the Council had cut the help by fifty per cent as the Society was considered "too ambitious" in its plans. One hopes that the events between that date and 1992 did not reflect a backward step in the Choir's repertoire. This was the last time that financial help came from this source which was later affected by cuts from the Government of the time for arts.

At Christmas in this year an experiment tried five years earlier, then unsuccessful, was again attempted to give the same concerts on two successive nights: Central Church, Torquay and All Saints Church, Brixham. Both events were successful. In the meantime extensive enquiries were being made for the cost of coaches, and even at one stage charting a private aircraft, for the trip to Hellevoetsluis, Holland in 1992. In the end, the visit had to be abandoned. The reasons were: a poor response from the members, the inability of teacher singer members to get time-off from school and the long travel arrangements by coach.

In June, 1992, *Carmina Burana* was again performed by the Society after a five years' gap. During this period this work, which had for many years been relatively unknown, suddenly gained popularity. The opening chorus of *O Fortuna* was used very often, and still is, as background music for commercial advertisements or dramatic images on the television screen. The English Riviera Centre was booked and Marilyn Hill-Smith with a fellow singer, Robert Carpenter Turner, from the popular radio BBC2 programme 'Friday Night is Music Night', were engaged as soloists and local television personality, Keith Fordyce, was to act as compère for the concert. A week later a number of members from the choir, together with the Royal British Legion Band, gave a concert in the Plymouth Athenaeum Theatre in Plymouth for the International Co-operative Day Rally. Sue Merryweather, the Society Accompanist, agreed to conduct the concert, which was arranged as a gesture of appreciation to this major sponsor of the Society.

AGMs can be boring events, particularly the Treasurer's report, if you are a regular sufferer. On a lighter note: at such a meeting in the Summer of 1992, the Treasurer reported that subscriptions showed that the Society had one hundred and sixteen point eight five members! A satisfactory explanation was, however, provided that the odd number did include 'casual singers' who supplemented certain concerts. This AGM did provide a legal problem in that it was not possible to find a new person willing to act as Treasurer. This was still not resolved at the Committee meeting in July following the AGM and Committee members discussed whether a person outside the Society membership should be sought through payment of an honorarium. A decision was also made to appoint an Assistant Chorusmaster/Conductor to cover for the Director of Music who, during the coming year, had a number of work official engagements which clashed with the Society rehearsals.

On 21 July, 1992, the Society once again acted as sponsor, this time for the Devon Youth Orchestra which performed at the Torquay Town Hall. A profit of £300 on this occasion was made and this was shared between the Orchestra and the Society. For the November concert in that year, the Committee thought big with a plan to use Exeter Cathedral for the *Dream of Gerontius*. Aware of the fact that the Paignton Choral Society followers might not be prepared to travel to Exeter to support the choir, the Committee felt that the prestige of performing in a cathedral venue might compensate for this gamble. Coaches from Torquay were provided for the choir and audience and there was a good attendance in the Cathedral. A month before this concert the Society appointed an Assistant Chorusmaster/Conductor, Christopher Fletcher, local music teacher, tutor and church organist, as agreed at the AGM. His first engagement was to conduct the Society Carol Concert on 5 December and the subsequent Civic Carol Concert at the English Riviera Centre to which the choir was again invited.

Early in 1993, warning was issued by the two people now acting as temporary Treasurers, that substantial deficits would result from the two 'Pomp and Circumstance' concerts planned. These were to be held at Central Church in March and All Saints Church, Brixham, in June. The latter concert marked the two hundredth anniversary of the birth of Henry F Lyte, famous for the hymn *Abide with me* and his association with that Church. The content of both concerts contained music used on Royal occasions and celebrated the fortieth year of the Queen's Accession to the Throne. Because of the financial situation, which had involved a £2,000 loan from a Society member, a planned concert of the choral version of *Carmen* was abandoned. The state of the accounts, however, improved slightly following the two concerts mentioned previously and was further helped by a £400 grant from South West Arts and £240 from the Plymouth Co-operative dividend stamps donated at a Paignton store. With a changed programme, the Society ventured into the countryside outside Torbay and almost filled a third of the Village Hall at Abbotskerswell with performers leaving not a lot of room for audience!

For the first concert of the 1993/4 season, Britten's *St Nicolas* made a re-appearance in the Society's programme together with the Haydn *Nelson Mass*. Students from St Cuthbert Mayne Junior School Choir, Torquay, joined the adult chorus in *St Nicolas*. The Society repeated the *Mass* at St

Mary's Church, Totnes, when it was included in the Eucharist Service on All Saints Day. Throughout the preceding months Society members were building up their enthusiasm at the prospect of a prestigious Christmas concert in the Festival Theatre with the Band of Her Majesty's Royal Marine Commandos Lympstone, near Exeter. Because of the political problems in Northern Ireland, the security of the Band at the time necessitated a complete search of the Theatre by police and sniffer dogs on the morning of the concert. Parking in the adjacent promenade was cancelled for the day, probably to the annoyance of Christmas shoppers who used the area for free parking. Police officers were stationed at every entrance to the Theatre for the Sunday evening performance and audience members' belongings were searched where appropriate. This huge involvement by the Devon & Cornwall Constabulary looked, at one stage, to have the Society involved in costs of between £2,000 and £5,000. However, after correspondence had taken place with the Chief Constable, he agreed to waive the costs as the Society was giving a charity performance for the Royal British Legion. A sigh of relief was sounded at the news, although the cost of the Band at £3,290 still had to be met. The Christmas concert, as one could imagine, was extremely successful performance-wise, but was a financial disaster despite eight hundred tickets being sold. Further, following the concert there was also considerable dispute with the firm who managed the Theatre on behalf of the Council, Apollo, regarding charges for various items of service. Given the large deficit the Society was facing, the Royal Marine Band was asked if it would make a donation from its own funds. This was not possible and, in the end, only a small refund was made by Apollo from the original quoted costs. The Society had hoped to make a large donation to the local branch of the Royal British Legion Poppy Appeal. However, once the loss on the concert had been calculated, only a £100 token payment could be made to the Appeal. Because of another work commitment for Mr Batten, Mr Fletcher conducted the Choir at the Theatre.

In June, 1994, the Society again returned to the Village Hall in Abbotskerswell, one week before their concert in the Torquay Town Hall. This rural concert was almost used as a public dress rehearsal for the larger event. Both performances included extracts from the *Pirates of Penzance* and *Les Misérables* as well as other pop-classics all under the concert titles 'Midsummer Music'. It was hoped that these two popular appeal concerts would help reduce the deficit incurred earlier in the season. This was the first time that the Town Hall Assembly Rooms had been used by the Society for one of their own concerts. The choir linked the concert with the one hundred and fiftieth anniversary of the Co-operative Movement's first shop, opened in 1844, as well as celebrating National Music Day. Together with local Directors of the Plymouth & South Devon Co-operative Society, Baroness Trumpington was present as the National Music Day Organising Committee's representative. Her ears must have needed some re-tuning as she had attended a Heavy Metal Concert at Dartmoor Prison the same afternoon!

By the Autumn of 1994 the Society's oldest singing member, a nonagenarian, Nelly Elmsdale, who had to stand down a year or so earlier from singing because of infirmity, was awarded an Honorary Life Membership. The new season saw a revision of the Society's rules which contained a number of ambiguities, and a replacement for Mr Fletcher following his resignation. Another Christopher, Christopher Sears FRCO, Head of Music at Torquay Boys' Grammar School and Organist/Choirmaster at All Saints Church, Babbacombe, Torquay, was appointed to the post at the AGM to start his duties from September, 1994. £600 was awarded to the Society by South West Arts to assist with the finances for the season.

In October, 1994, a new initiative sponsored by British Telecom, in which the Paignton Choral Society participated, came into being when *Messiah* concerts simultaneously took place in aid of hospices. Over two hundred in this country, and fifty performances elsewhere in the world, were given. The local event supported Rowcroft Hospice in Torquay. Yet again, another new church was used for the Haydn concert the following month, this time at the other end of the area. St Mary the Virgin Parish Church, St Marychurch, Torquay was the venue and for the Spring concert St Luke's Church, Torquay was used for only the second time. Both churches presented staging problems because of the current size of the choir and fixed choir stalls in the chancel area.

At South Devon College in February, 1995, a dinner served by students in the Hotel and Catering Department was the first of a number of social events held at this venue by the choir. In May a small number of choir members formed themselves into a group and gave a concert of light music mixed with a little magic from the Choir Secretary. This event, held at the Palace Avenue Theatre, was for the Co-operative Women's Guild Annual Congress in Torquay. Two choirs, the Gloucester Choral Society and Plymouth Philharmonic Choir, joined the Paignton Society to perform *Balshazzar's Feast* in June, both having sung it the previous year, although locally it was a 'first'.

At this point another innovative idea for raising funds was organized by a member of the Choir, Doreen Gahan. An old-fashioned wind-up alarm clock was placed in a sealed box, and time spaces bought for when the participant thought the clock would stop. Good prizes were obtained for the three nearest predictions and just over two hundred and fifty pounds profit was made.

At the well-attended performance of *Elijah* in November, 1995, a survey of audience views about timing of concerts, sources from which tickets had been obtained, advertising methods, transport arrangements and programme content was organized. A similar survey amongst choir members was also conducted. A complete renovation of the Society piano faced members and to raise funds for this a 'buy a piano note key' fund was started.

Much of the Committee's discussion during the latter part of 1995 and for many months up to June 1996 was dominated by plans for the Verdi concert at the Riviera Centre (as it was now known), Torquay. With invited members from the Harborne Singers, Totnes, Plymouth Philharmonic Choir and the Truro Choral Society, a plan had to be drawn up for the *Requiem* in order to accommodate two hundred choir members and an eighty-strong orchestra. Special staging and advertising, as well as the big challenges for all who were involved, not least the £8,000 cost of putting on the work, were having to be faced. Unfortunately, difficulties were experienced with the Centre's box-office computer arrangements which, in the opinion of the Committee, resulted in poor ticket sales and a smaller audience than had been anticipated. Musically the concert was excellent.

At the Committee meeting in June before the AGM, the problems noticed at the end of the financial year in May were highlighted. The end of a Society's financial year usually showed a large sum being carried over before the final concert in June or July. It was felt that this gave a false picture of the true financial situation at the end of a season and could also affect applications for grant-aid or sponsorship. It was decided that this matter would be aired at the AGM and appropriate action taken, if agreed by members, to change the end-of-year accounts to a later date.

For the 'Sing Noel' concert in the same year, 1996, the Society 'took over' a much smaller church than usual, the Newton Abbot Methodist Church in Avenue Road. With the Newton Abbot Junior Music Centre Orchestra and a large choir squashed into a small area of the Church, a packed audience was guaranteed and duly materialized.

The Extra-ordinary meeting of the Society called in January, 1997, approved the changes to the rules and constitution, which had also been agreed by the Charity Commissioners. Most important was that the Society's financial year would in future be moved to the end of August of each year. With the AGM now in January, time could be allowed for the Treasurer to balance the accounts and have them audited. The change of the date also gave time to appoint a new Director of Music if the normal twelve months notice had been given that he or she wished to stand down at the end of the season. By May, 1997, the need for an Assistant Accompanist was also identified and Mrs Val Wood was appointed for the beginning of the following season.

The Summer concert of June, 1997, provided an interesting challenge for the Society. Something out of the ordinary took place when Dyson's *Canterbury Pilgrims* was performed. This work had somewhat faded into oblivion in the music world in recent years, although a record company had recently revived interest in it by producing a compact disc of the work. The performance also coincided with the anniversary, fourteen hundred years earlier, of the arrival of St Augustine in 597. The Dean of Canterbury Cathedral responded to a letter sent to him notifying him of the concert and expressed his good wishes and success for the event. To encourage interest in it, a prize competition was offered to local school children to design pictures depicting the key characters in 'Chaucer's Tales' on which the music was based. A number of primary schools took part and one hundred and forty drawings were received. Financially, the Director for Arts and Recreation of Torbay Council, Bob Sweet, gave substantial support to the Society by obtaining concessions on the normal hire charge of the Festival Theatre. In recognition of his help, assistance with the use of Council staging and his general interest in the activities of the Society over the years, a Life Membership was awarded to him.

The Society was invited to take part in the Seventy-fifth Anniversary of the St John Ambulance Service in Devon in October, 1997 as the Exeter Cathedral Choir was not available for the event. In addition to the anthem *Hail Gladdening Light* by Charles Wood, two extracts from the *Messiah* were included. This was a good opportunity for the latter items to be performed prior to the second Triennial British telecom 'Voices for Hospices Messiah' with the Paignton Choral Society this time acting as the 'lead' choir. The Festival Theatre was selected for this event with a large gathering of about two hundred, including invited singers, and forty orchestral members. The large ensemble necessitated extension of the stage with the removal of some of the seating at the front of the auditorium. For the Christmas 'Sing Noel' concert the Devon Youth Orchestra joined the Choir for the performance in the Torquay Town Hall Assembly Rooms.

In January, 1998, the first AGM was held in accordance with the changed constitution. This enabled the Society to provide accounts embracing the whole of a choir season, to appoint music staff, Committee officers and members from the beginning of the next choir season. It also provided plenty of time to seek replacements for resignations or outstanding vacancies (if they were not filled at the AGM) over a period of eight months. This year also saw the Society again co-operating with other groups for a joint event, the first of which was the *Dream of Gerontius*. Plymouth Philharmonic Choir, which had sung the work the year before, swelled the choir to two hundred singers for the performance in the Torquay Town Hall

Assembly Rooms. This was the only suitable venue in the area for a choir of this size without the need for the Society to incur considerable costs.

A suggestion made in 1990 at the joint meeting with Torbay Singers Committee members for a local co-ordinated music diary, was again raised at the February, 1998 Committee meeting of the Choral Society. This was seen as a way to overcome some of the problems of duplication of dates, and even works, which were occurring locally. It was also felt that many similar groups to the Choral Society were often chasing the same audiences. The Secretary of the Society and author of this book volunteered to create a quarterly diary. Initially seven groups in the South Devon area agreed to participate. This did not involve any cost to them other than a supply of stamped-addressed envelopes to post back the current edition to a named person in the group. Copies would also be sent to local media and information points. To help with the costs of 'Musical Notes', the name given to the diary, a grant was secured from two local councils to cover postage to the media and general stationery costs in its production. As knowledge of the diary spread, the societies wishing to be included expanded outside the local area.

On the 18 July, 1998, the Society and the Truro Choral Society gave the first major classical music concert in the 'New Hall for Cornwall', Truro. This hall had opened only twelve months before. Two coaches containing thirty audience members plus some choir singers and their friends travelled down from Torbay for the *Carmina Burana* performance. They competed on the congested roads with other travellers including holiday visitors and people attending the 'Tall Ships Race' in Falmouth. Despite this, the participating choir singers managed to arrive in Truro in good time for rehearsal and performance.

For November an evening devoted to the work of Beethoven and featuring his *Mass in C* was arranged, and a brilliant young pianist, Lada Valasova, who had studied music at the Prague Conservatoire and Music Academy, played the *Piano concerto No 3 in C minor*. In addition to the Christmas concert given in the Torquay Town Hall Assembly Rooms, the Society was again invited to take part in a Christmas concert in Exeter Cathedral with two local school choirs. This time it was held to celebrate an anniversary of the National Trust.

Whilst the Society enjoyed a concert in the brand new hall in Truro, a loss was felt in Paignton. On 2 and 3 January, 1999, Cinderella dropped her glass slipper for the final time in the Festival Theatre, Paignton. The Russian Ice Stars Company presenting 'Cinderella on Ice' was the last to use the stage. Under its Apollo Management the Festival Theatre was to be converted into a multi-screen complex which opened later in the year following major building alterations. As recorded previously, on many occasions since it first opened in June, 1967, the Theatre had been used by the Society for concerts. With the exception of the Riviera Centre, which was not really a concert hall and Princess Theatre which was costly to hire, the loss of the Festival Theatre would restrict the Paignton Choral Society in finding venues for further big concerts and where large audiences could be seated.

At the March, 1999, Committee meeting it was decided that it would be helpful to explore new locations for a concert. The Newton Abbot area was considered, although suitable venues still presented a problem. In the end, St Mary's Church, Abbotsbury appeared to have the flexibility on the church floor for a performance of Vivaldi's *Gloria* and other choral works.

Two months later, in May, following planning for over a year, a party of singers, relations and friends and a small orchestra boarded a double-decked coach for Caen, Normandy, to repeat the *Gloria*. With glorious weather enhancing the visit the main performance was given in the Church of St Peter in the centre of the city as part of the Mass service, and the complete work was sung the following day in a small church in the rural outskirts of Caen. The singers and orchestra almost outnumbered the audience but the hospitality buffet by the hosts after the concert was superb. One month later another new work to the Society was performed when Vaughan Williams' *Cotswold Romance* was presented along with the first half of the programme devoted to opera chorus favourites.

In September, 1999, it is believed that for the first time, the Committee decided to appoint an Orchestral Secretary outside the Society membership and to pay an honorarium. Michael Merryweather, husband of the Society Accompanist, took on the role. This was a great help because he was a musician himself, music teacher/tutor and could use the many contacts he had with other professionals in the same field. To end the century the Society sang in the original language Brahms' *German Requiem*, at Central Church. A previous performance of this work, then sung in English, had been given in November, 1974. Finally, the Society returned to its traditional 'Sing Noel' which, this time, was taken over to the other end of Torbay and performed at All Saints Church, Brixham.

2000 - 2012

CHAPTER 4 OF THIS history of the Paignton and South Devon Choral Society commences in the Millennium Year, with the appointment of a President after a seventeen year gap since Norman del Mar had occupied the post. Vincent McCann, Mayor of Torbay from 1998 to 1999, who was a regular member in the audience of the Choir's concerts and a valuable link with the Council in his capacity as a Borough Councillor until 2000, agreed to accept the Presidency of the Society.

The first concert of the year was in April with a return to Christ Church, Paignton, and the main work as Fauré's *Requiem*. The Conductor of the Truro Choral Society, Michael Edwards, conducted his own composition *Immortality* as part of the concert. Links had already been established with the Truro Society in 1998 when the Paignton singers travelled to that city to perform *Carmina Burana* with their members. As the first half of the year proceeded, preparations were already in progress for a visit by the French Choir 'Croque-Notes' from St Nazaire in July. This had evolved through another link between the Society's Conductor and his French counterpart. To assist with costs, a Millennium Festival 'Awards for All' bid through the National Lottery was successful and amounted to £1,671. This Anglo/French concert commenced with a special Millennium Fanfare written by a young former student, Christopher Leedham, of Torquay Boys' Grammar School who had moved on to Oxford University to read music and had been especially commissioned to write this work. In October the Berlioz *Te Deum* sung in July was repeated at the church in the centre of St Nazaire. Prior to that concert the third Triennial 'BT Voices for Hospices' performance of *Messiah* took place with the Society once again acting as the 'lead' choir in Torquay. Other singers from local choirs were invited to participate and this resulted in a chorus of one hundred and twenty performers.

To return to the visit to France: it was plain sailing, literally, out to the concert and the performance with some Choir members being hosted by the St Nazaire Choir. The return journey, however, was a nightmare in every sense of the word! In a gathering gale force wind, the Brittany Ferry left Roscoff on the Sunday afternoon in October. By 10.00pm it was due to dock in Plymouth, but as the wind force increased across the Channel and with the boat rocking violently it had to shelter in a bay outside the Breakwater in Plymouth Sound as it could not dock. Emergency berths were allocated to passengers if they needed them, although sleep must have been difficult with the pounding of the waves on the side of the stationary ship. Like many others, the author of this history opted for a reclining chair where at least one could see what was happening and fight off threatening sea-sickness. Alarmingly, in between fits of sleep, he thought he saw patterns of light on the coast line only for the same group to appear some short while later. It was not until the following day that it was learned that the Ferry had slipped one of its anchors and the boat had been swinging around in circles a number of times in the stormy seas. The Ferry finally docked at 9.00am the following morning escorted by a tug. To add to the chaos, members' cars parked in a school over the week end, blocked the teaching staff from parking their own cars when school assembled that morning!

The Millennium year ended for the Society at Central Church with a concert entitled 'An Evening with Mozart' and included his well-known *Requiem in D minor*. The rehearsals for this concert had a piano accompaniment by Sue Merryweather, as had the preparation for previous programmes since September, 1986, when she was appointed. She decided this would be her last concert and the post was offered to Christopher Sears, already Assistant Director of Music and Chorusmaster since 1994, to become the official Accompanist from January, 2001.

For the Spring 2001 concert using the title 'Music of Edwardian England' the Society members donned suitable Edwardian-style costumes in keeping with the fashions of that period and the theme of musical works to be performed. A publicity photograph was taken with a few members apparently singing around a piano in a typical early twentieth century public house in the local visitor history attraction 'Bygones' in Torquay.

The Society's Conductor, Mr Melvyn Batten, had held the position of Deputy Director of Devon Youth Music for seven years. The Society decided to mark the last occasion when he would conduct the Devon Youth Orchestra by sponsoring their concert at the Paignton Community College in April, 2001. Following this, another unique event for the Society was planned for July also to involve groups of young people. A grant of £962 was this time awarded by the Lottery 'Awards for All' Fund to assist with the expenses of bringing together seventy children from the older groups in primary and the younger students in secondary local schools. With gusto they sang Carter's *Benedicite*, a work specially written for young people. The concert ended with enthusiastic singing from parents, their off-springs, choir and audience in a highly popular song of the time, ABBA's well known piece "Thank you for the Music" which was also used for the title of the event.

Following the AGM in January, 2001, as the Society moved into the second season of the millennium year, a radical change took place for the third time in the Society's history. A new name was adopted to reflect the diverse area from which members came. The title 'South Devon Choir' was suggested amongst other names and agreed by the membership at the AGM. From now on the Society will be referred to as such in this history. A new title for the Choir had been considered in the 1990's, but was rejected at the time as some members, particularly Paigntonians, wished to retain the link with Paignton in the name.

A competition was also held for a new logo design using the name, and after some interesting art work had been displayed to members a clever design by Mr Gordon Batten was overwhelmingly selected. Along with both these changes in the Choir's image, the lady members replaced their traditional white angel-style tops for long black dress accompanied by bright red scarves with a music-note motif worn hanging round their shoulders. Perhaps fittingly, the first concert of the new season when the ladies wore their new dress was Haydn's *Creation!* In a review later of this concert, the old chestnut came up yet again about the lack of tenor and bass voices. The Director of Music suggested if a recruitment drive did not find singers in those sections, then to continue to sing four-part works extra singers would have to be brought in and their services paid for. He added that if there had been two fewer basses he would have cancelled the concert.

A month after the *Creation* performance, the Choir was invited to attend the Civic Carol Concert as guest choir at the Riviera Centre, Torquay, after a gap of ten years. The day after that concert, Friday, 14 December, the Choir's own Carol Concert, using the now well-established title 'Sing Noel', was taken to St Mary's Church, Abbotsbury, Newton Abbot. Pupils from a local primary school, Chudleigh Church of England School at which Mr Batten, the Choir's Conductor taught music, provided the orchestral items. Unfortunately, there were other competing Christmas events in the area and some of the usual 'following' of the Choir were reluctant to travel to Newton Abbot for a concert, and the audience attendance was not good.

Two further items need to be added to the record for the year 2001. The Committee discussed the need for more prominent publicity. The result of this was to buy a professional banner which gave the flexibility of plastic adhesive lettering which could be removed and replaced according to the content and date of a concert. Finally, the status of the President was recognized by a new badge displaying the Choir's new name and logo.

To start the New Year, 2002, the Secretary of the Choir and author of this book had compiled Part II of the Choir history (1946-1999), as fairly complete information through past minutes, programmes and newspaper articles was available to make the task easy. Copies were sold to members, but as further research later revealed the date of the Choir's foundation and much other related information have been incorporated into this book.

In examining the record of concerts performed by the Choir, the reader of this history will have noted that some works appeared regularly. By contrast, Dvořák's *Stabat Mater*, last sung twenty-four years earlier, was chosen for March, 2002. The Rossini version had been performed in 1996. *Stabat Mater* was performed as an appropriate choice for Good Friday. Four years earlier the Committee decided that a concert could sometimes be performed on this day, and in that year it was Stainer's *Crucifixion*. Instead of a usual Saturday concert, the Committee felt that Good Friday in Holy Week might attract good attendance as few events on that evening compete for audiences. The only problem arising from the choice of that day is that services often extend into the afternoon, resulting in a church not available until late in the day for the setting-up of seating prior to the choir's arrival. Appropriately, for *Stabat Mater*, the ladies of the Choir had purple scarves for the first time, purchased through the generosity of a Committee member.

Following the March concert, an exchange visit was again planned with the St Nazaire choir, 'Croque-Notes', but as they were able to come to England only over the August Bank Holiday, it was decided to abandon the idea. Ferry problems and the lack of interest from members during a period when the Choir is normally in recess, added to the difficulties for an exchange. On a different issue: to encourage membership sales, for the next concert a new policy was adopted by inserting two tickets inside each member's score. The hope was that it might encourage the members to sell a minimum of two seats and ideally ask for more tickets.

At this stage Christopher Sears, the Assistant Director of Music and Chorusmaster, had not conducted the Choir at one of its own concerts. The previous Christmas he had taken up the baton for the celebrations at the Civic Carol Concert mentioned earlier. Under the title 'Jubilate Deo', when the Queen's Golden Jubilee in June was being nationally celebrated, a varied programme of works, many used on royal and ceremonial occasions, was given at Christopher's own Church, All Saints, Babbacombe, Torquay, where he was Organist and Choirmaster.

By November, 2002, the Choir's earlier problems returned, when the Conductor expressed concern about key soprano singers unable to attend the *Elijah* concert. Attempts were made to gain the assistance from other local choirs and in the end some singers were recruited from the Stanborough Chorus, a Kingsbridge-based choir. This was the start of a close friendship with the Chorus which was to develop, as we shall see, in 2004. For the performance of *Elijah* a student from Torquay Boys' Grammar School sang the young *Elijah* solos and some girls from Teign School, Kingsteignton, Newton Abbot, formed the sub-chorus. At the same time a language student from Germany was in Torquay and asked if she might attend rehearsals for a short while to improve her English. This prompted the idea to send a general publicity leaflet to the larger Language Schools in Torbay to invite their students to come along to the Choir rehearsals if they enjoyed classical music. As a gesture to the Plymouth and South Devon Co-operative Society, which had made annual grants of £1,000 to the Choir since 1991, a small group of members sang carols to shoppers in the Newton Abbot store to raise money for that Society's adopted annual charity.

Some of the works of the very popular, modern composer, John Rutter, well known for arranging music for children and amateur choirs, featured in the March, 2003 concert. A personal letter was received from the composer in which he said: "I am delighted that my Requiem is featured in tonight's concert by the South Devon Choir, together with my shorter pieces. When I wrote this in memory of my father in 1985, I probably thought it would receive one performance, but my publisher and I soon found it was being sung by choirs all over the world. All of us, of course, experience loss and bereavement at some time in our lives, and I hope in the words and music of this work, some light and consolation may be found. I send my best wishes for a happy and successful concert".

In September, 2003, a husband-and-wife team in the Choir who were also Vice-Presidents, were soon to leave the area. In recognition of the service they had given, they were made Life Members. Howard Leaman had been Chairperson from 1970-1972 and his wife, Pat, Orchestral Secretary for many years. Both had been involved in key Choir activities over the years. At the same Committee meeting in that month, Alan Hawkins, a Trustee and Treasurer at the United Reformed Congregational Church, Paignton, at which the Choir rehearsed, warned that with falling congregations the Church might close in the future.

As preparation for a performance of the Schubert *Deutches Messe* in November, to be sung in German, (yet again a 'first' for the Choir), Guy Palmer, Head of German at the Torquay Boys' Grammar School, was invited to one of the rehearsals to give the Choir a lesson in the pronunciation of the words.

During the Christmas shopping period a visit was again made to the Co-operative store for carol singing to raise funds for their adopted charity.

At this point it is important to side-track and record the important big plans and negotiations taking place in Committee. As a result of a long-standing friendship between the Treasurer of the North Devon Choral

Society and a member of the South Devon Choir and her husband (Sally and Brian Laird), a suggestion was made that the two Choirs again join forces. Because the North Devon Choral Society had sung with the Paignton Choral Society (as it was known then) in Quimper, France, in 1989 and 1990, the offer was readily taken up. The North Devon Choral Society had performed the Verdi *Requiem* in 2002 celebrating their Golden Jubilee, and this work was the choice. In one of many joint meetings with Directors of Music and key Committee members of both choirs, it was agreed this would be performed again. The South Devon Choir already had links with the Stanborough Chorus, and as they would have been unable to present a work of this magnitude on their own, they indicated they would be delighted to become the third part to be involved. The resulting potential of two hundred and fifty singers, an orchestra, professional soloists and an estimated cost of £15,000 for two concerts in North and South Devon was a daunting project. The choice of venue to use in South Devon, the Torquay Assembly Rooms in the Town Hall, was fairly obvious, as this was really the only location which could accommodate a choir of this size, an orchestra and audience. Other alternatives would have been the Riviera Centre and the Princess Theatre, both of which would have added a minimum of £2,000 to the concert costs before box office and other built-in expenses were added. The Stanborough Chorus had no suitable place in South Hams in which they could host a concert. In North Devon two churches were considered but, as in most religious buildings, the problem of fixed furniture in the altar area created problems. A suggestion to use the Barnstaple Pannier Market eventually emerged and appeared worthy of investigation, especially as the concert in that area was planned for a Sunday. Heating, lighting, closure of the adjacent public thoroughfare to the Market (Butcher's Row) with a police presence, hire of nine hundred seats, the building of staging additional to that which was already owned by the North Devon Choral Society, changing-accommodation for the choirs, orchestra and soloists, a ticket agency … were just some of the issues to be faced.

To prepare for these two mammoth *Verdi* concerts, the South Devon Choir organized a special event at an unusual venue. In 1987, the Torquay Operatic and Dramatic Society Company, TOADS as they are known, obtained planning consent and listed building approval clearance to change the interior of a redundant Church of England Church to an entertainment venue. Steeply-tiered seats for an audience of up to two hundred and thirty nine in number were built in the nave area and the altar area was converted into a stage. At a cost of £250,000, other areas of the former church were converted into dressing rooms, foyer, box office and a café. In 1998 TOADS gave their first performance in this now intimate, cosy, theatre named the Little Theatre. This was an ideal location for the Choir to hold its first Workshop, bearing in mind the numbers likely to attend. Members of the three Choirs were invited to take part as were other singers who, if they felt competent to do so, were given the chance to perform in both concerts or either. A total of one hundred and sixteen people participated in the Workshop, and a small number of singers outside the three choirs took advantage of the concert performance offer. A grant of £200 from the National Federation of Music Societies (South-West) was made towards the cost of the event, and John Hobbs directed it. Already Director of Music for the North Devon Choral Society, three years later he was to be appointed to the same post for the South Devon Choir.

On 20 March, 2004, with the massed choirs (named the '3CD's – 3 Choirs of Devon') numbering two hundred and thirteen, four soloists and a large orchestra, the first concert was given in front of an audience of about four hundred. A similar-sized audience, with all the organisational problems overcome, listened the following day to the late Sunday afternoon Verdi *Requiem* concert in the Pannier Market in North Devon. We understand that this was a unique experience for the Market. This was the first time it had been used for a classical music concert since it was built in 1885. The financial gamble taken by the three Choirs paid off, much to the working- party's relief, and a small deficit was met proportionally by each group. To add some amusing riders to the whole venture in North Devon, although not for the persons concerned, the Stage Manager, who was a farmer, trundled his way back in his tractor after the concert with the staging loaded on a trailer. He had to stop a mile from his home where the staging was stored, because his neighbour's bullocks had strayed into the lane blocking his way. Having rounded them up, he proceeded on his journey. To add to his exhausting day, further troubles developed a few minutes later when his trailer sustained a tyre puncture! In another episode that day, a South Devon Choir member parked his car in a local Barnstaple car-park only to find the place locked up at 6.00pm. The following day he had to make the one hundred and twenty mile round trip to retrieve his vehicle when the car-park re-opened.

The Summer concert 2004 saw a return to All Saints Church, Babacombe, Torquay, the home-ground of Christopher Sears, when he conducted a programme of well-known choral classics. The services of the Head

Chorister from Exeter Cathedral were commissioned for "O for the Wings of a Dove" in Mendelssohn's famous work *Hear my Prayer*.

The developments of modern technology affect every part of the lives of people and workings of organizations and the South Devon Choir Committee felt it should not be an exception. In the 2004 season the idea of setting up a website for the Choir was suggested. This would enable members of the public to log-on for details of concerts. For potential new singers and residents to the area a main page would contain a photograph and some historical background of the Choir. Subsequent pages could show Officers' contact details, rehearsal venue information, subscription charges, audition requirement (if appropriate) and other facts. Investigations were to take place as to how this could be created and to learn from the experiences of other local societies which already had websites.

A 'Music Entente Cordiale' title was used for an Anglo/French programme of music at the start of the 2004/5 season. In Britten's *St Nicolas* the use of young people in a concert was again achieved. Three 'pickle boys' for the work were recruited from the local Boys' Grammar School and Patricia Sears, wife of the Assistant Director of Music, Christopher Sears, trained a sub-chorus from the South Devon Music Centre.

By the New Year, the dress for the men in the Choir had been enhanced by the addition of bow ties in red and light blue to match the ladies' scarves when worn in those colours at a concert.

At this stage a leap back of three years is necessary. It has already been mentioned how social contacts can stimulate all sorts of future events as shown in the case of the Verdi *Requiem* performances in 2004. This time a chance social chat across a north of England bar took place by Douglas, a former Treasurer of the Choir and husband to Margaret Johnstone who was a Choir member and soloist soprano often invited to sing in concerts. His fellow drinker was from the North Yorkshire Chorus and conversation led to a discussion about music. From that meeting, at various stages, plans began to evolve for an exchange finally fixed for 2005. By early Spring of that year details were being finalized for the visit of the Chorus to Torquay and the return visit by the South Devon choir to Ripon. The arrangements included the matching of hosts with visiting singers, independent accommodation where required, travel and singing numbers. The selection of the work, Vaughan Williams' *A Sea Symphony* was appropriately linked with a National theme of 'The Year of the Sea' which also co-incided with the two hundredth anniversary of the Battle of Trafalgar. Preceding the concert a local Choral Workshop was again arranged in the Little Theatre, Torquay. The services of the Director of Music for the North Yorkshire Chorus were obtained to take the workshop, although numbers attending this time were less with forty-one South Devon Choir members present and thirty-six external singers. A £200 grant from NFMS (South West) was again awarded towards the tutor's fee.

With a good audience attendance at Central Church, Torquay, sixty-eight South Devon choir and thirty-one singers from the North Yorkshire Chorus performed *A Sea Symphony* at the end of April. A grant of £775, this time from the Lottery 'Awards for All', was obtained to cover the fees of young music students playing in the orchestra and the fee of a young baritone, Nicholas Merryweather. Nicholas was in the early stages of his professional career and the son of Sue Merryweather, who was the Choir Accompanist from 1986 to 2000, and Michael Merryweather, who was to become Orchestral Secretary in 1999. During the concert, an unfortunate accident occurred involving a bass seated in the rear row on the stage of Central Church, a case of 'man overboard', bearing in mind the title of one of the main works being performed. The summoning of an ambulance and the halting of the concert resulted in a loss of impetus and atmosphere which were being created in the music. Fortunately, the bass suffered only bruising to his body and after hospital treatment returned to Choir several weeks later.

On the 14 May, thirty-six singers made the return visit to Ripon, some travelling by a coach which had been booked, and others in private cars. A small number of friends and partners from South Devon also made the trip. Performing in the grandeur of Ripon Cathedral gave the performance a special atmosphere. Students from the Symphony Orchestra at Sheffield University, for which the Conductor of the North Yorkshire Chorus was the Director of Performance, accompanied the *Sea Symphony*. For both visits singers and some partners stayed in bed-and-breakfast accommodation or as guests of the 'home' choir. As far as all exchanges and links with other choirs are concerned, the value of these cannot be over-stated. A great number of lasting friendships are created with people who enjoy at least one common interest – choral singing.

By October the Choir had made use of modern technology and a website had been set up with the help of a local computer expert. Purchase of some redundant spotlights from a local theatre company had also been made and investigations were being undertaken for sources from which stands and cabling could be purchased. In November the Torquay Brass Band invited the Choir to join in a 'Last Night of the Proms' finale of their concert and two weeks later an Italian-themed concert with Puccini's *Messa di Gloria* and some well-known opera choruses by composers of that country was given by the Choir. To gain free advance publicity – something like gold dust at times – it often pays to come up with something out of the ordinary, a pure gimmick, which might catch the eye of the local newspaper editor and even get a photographer along. The idea of a few members of the Committee apparently going to an Italian Restaurant for a meal to plan the final details of the concert achieved the required publicity with a photograph in the 'Herald Express.'

Mind you, the Committee quite enjoyed the meal as well! Finally, for the 2004/5 season an unscheduled performance conducted by Christopher Sears at All Saints Church, Babbacombe, Torquay, was included in the Choir's programme. This resulted from the local Rotary Club's lack of success in gaining support for a one day 'Come & Sing' event, with the South Devon Choir taking over the responsibility with normal rehearsals and a concert. One of the Rotary Club's sponsored charities was supported and £424 was donated to the Children's Hospice South West.

In his report at the AGM in January, 2006, the Director of Music, Melvyn Batten, made a statement which, to many, may seem highly controversial. He stated: "there was a saying that choral societies should always be in the red which indicated they were using music to the maximum". Over a number of years for the South Devon Choir that had certainly been true – in the red – with deficits at the end of the financial year requiring sometimes an interest free-loan from members of the Choir to tide the society over. At the same meeting, Alan Hawkins, who had warned three years previously that the United Reformed Church in Paignton might close because of falling congregations, stated that this would finally happen in July 2006. With this news the Committee started to investigate alternative venues. Consideration had to be given to the size of a new rehearsal hall bearing in mind the Choir numbers, location, parking, kitchen and disabled facilities and access. The hall had to be available on a Thursday night which it was felt most members ear-marked as 'choir night'. Added to this was the problem that where the Choir went the piano had to come too! A move would also involve the possible sale of chairs which the Choir owned and were used in the current Church rehearsal hall, and part-disposal of a cupboard and music accumulated over many years.

Returning to finance for a moment, a novel way of raising money materialized through a 'Promises Auction' organized in March. With the offer of services using the skills of Choir members which included: hosting a meal for four; a horse-riding lesson; a conjuring show; an afternoon sail. With additional gifts from businesses, members and their friends bid for the lots as they came under the hammer. An amazing sum of over £1,000 was raised in a couple of hours at a local hostelry using a professional auctioneer - a relation of one of the Choir members. In the same month a third workshop was held with one hundred and thirteen people attending. *The Dream of Gerontius* was to be performed the following month. The Choir again linked with the Stanborough Chorus which celebrated its twentieth anniversary and Melvyn Batten conducted the combined forces for this work. He rated this amongst his top ten favourite oratorios. Also in March, Mr Batten indicated to the Committee that he now felt that the time had been reached for his departure as Director of Music, and that a new person should be sought for the Choir from September 2007.

By the end of the year the Committee had reached several useful decisions and changes. Following the death in March of Angela Barton, a former Choir member who had been suffering from deteriorating health for a number of years, the Committee learnt that a generous legacy of £1,500 had been given to the Choir. After debate, the Director of Music suggested that one concert, known as the 'Angela Barton Memorial Concert', every alternate year should be allocated £500 from the fund. Any accumulated money through interest could be devoted to a fourth concert. The idea was warmly accepted by Angela's husband, Paul. The second decision after a number of enquiries and viewings, was that the Choir, with its piano, would move into the hall at the Hollacombe Community Resources Centre, Paignton, from September 2006. The final notes to add to this paragraph are that the Choir's website was finally up and running, and that a Life Membership was bestowed on Alan Hawkins. As Covenant/Gift-aid Secretary he had brought in hundreds of pounds into the accounts, and as Trustee at the Paignton United Reformed Church he had been a useful link for use of the Hall. Unfortunately, immobility had prevented his attendance at the Choir for some time.

By October, 2006, the Choir had settled into its new rehearsal hall and appointing a new Director of Music was underway. With the vacancy advertised on several websites on the Internet, enquiries were received from places as far afield as Slovakia, France, the Netherlands, Germany and even Nigeria. Most of these were impracticable unless the applicant had another income to enable him or her to remain in this country. Local response was disappointing and known key people were identified and discreetly approached to see if they were interested.

The following month the first 'Angela Barton Memorial Fund' concert was held. At the Brahms *German Requiem* performance a pianist, Lada Valasova, who had now gained international recognition, played the Grieg *Piano Concerto in A minor*. She had appeared previously with the Choir in November, 1998, in the early stages of her professional career. To round off the year, the Choir was again guest choir at the Civic Carol Concert in the Riviera Centre in December.

Following the interview of four local candidates who had also conducted in turn a short piece at a choir rehearsal, a decision was reached at a Special

Committee meeting on 22 January, 2007, to appoint John Hobbs as Director of Music from September, 2007. His association with the Choir stretched over many years as a soloist and he was already conducting the North Devon and Bude Choral Societies. In making the appointment, there were some slight concerns that he could find the weekly travel from his home in the Bideford area to Torbay too arduous especially in inclement weather.

For Mr Batten's 'swan-song' departure a performance of *Messiah* was arranged, and several soloists asked to be included in this special farewell event. The significance of this concert was indicated by the large audience of two hundred and eighty plus orchestra and choir, stretching the capacity of the Central Church to the full extent. At the final rehearsal a Life Membership of the Choir was given to Mr Batten together with a loose-leaf book of members' reminiscences of his twenty-one years with the Choir. A buffet for Choir members and friends was arranged after the *Messiah* concert as a formal way to say "au revoir".

In 2007, the time was coming around for the second 3CD concert. The planning group had met a number of times during the previous year. For the agreed performance of Orff's *Carmina Burana*, Rosemary Cole, Director of Music for the Stanborough Chorus, conducted the three choirs and John Hobbs conducted the first half with a Mendelssohn work. In preparation for this concert the Little Theatre in Torquay was again used for a workshop with fifty-two singers from the South Devon Choir attending (fewer than last time), twenty six from the Stanborough Chorus and eleven guest singers. The Torquay Town Hall was again used as the venue for the massed voices on the Saturday, followed by the Sunday afternoon concert in the Barnstaple Pannier Market (complete with pigeons flying around the rafters!). A slightly disconcerting element occurred when a peel of bells summoning parishioners to the nearby church rang out during the beautiful "In Trutina" near the end of *Carmina Burana*. The soprano, Heloise West, however, continued undeterred. With an adult chorus of about one hundred and seventy at each concert, girls from Stoodley Knowle Convent and Kingsbridge Community College sang the sub-choruses in the work at Torquay, and Bideford and Braunton Community Colleges at Barnstaple. Unfortunately, with smaller audience attendance at both concerts, the three Choirs had to share a loss of over £10,000.

By September, 2007, Mr Hobbs had commenced his duties as Director of Music in South Devon, and a new replacement Orchestral Secretary was sought for Michael Merryweather, who had given excellent service over eight years to the Choir. Following the sad death of the Choir President, Vince McCann, in April and his funeral in May, at which a number of Choir members sang, a donation was made to the Choir in his memory by his long-time friend, Tony Satchwell. The money was used to purchase the valuable asset of stands and cabling for the Choir floodlights previously purchased in October 2005.

For the first concert Mr Hobbs introduced the Choir to Bach's *Christmas Oratorio*. This had not been sung since 1982 and this was the first of many occasions with Mr Hobbs challenging the Choir with more unfamiliar or new works. Some Choir members returned to the Plymouth & SW Co-operative Homemaker store in December for carol singing in aid of its adopted charity, the Devon Air Ambulance. At the AGM in January the following year, the members were asked to approve the Committee's suggestion that Mike Thompson, former Deputy Editor of the 'Herald Express', be appointed as the Choir's new President. Because of his support to the Choir over the years and as a well-known personality in the community, the appointment seemed ideal. Appropriately, his favourite composer Elgar was to be included in the next concert.

Over subsequent Committee meetings, and after a lapse of many years, an attractive brochure to advertise the season's concerts was prepared by a computer 'wizard' Choir member, John Christian. He had also been instrumental in taking many photographs and recordings of the Choir and his valuable help in preparing this book, with others, has already been recorded. With one thousand copies distributed to key points such as libraries, information/tourist centres, local music shops and other venues it was hoped larger audiences might be attracted to concerts. The Committee also reviewed the 'Friends of the Choir' membership and how to increase it, as well as which other benefits could be offered to people joining that group.

The July, 2008, concert was interesting in the fact that Coleridge Taylor's *Hiawatha's Wedding Feast* re-appeared in the programme for the first time since 1968. In the late 1940's, when the work had been included, students from local dancing schools had performed a ballet sequence. At the 2008 concert under what some might consider a 'tongue-in-cheek' title, 'Rats to Hiawatha', the dance of Pau-Puk-Keewis was given by a talented young student, Georgia O'Reilly, who was attending the Royal Ballet School. The 'Rats' title was used because the *Pied Piper of Hamelin* by Parry was also included in the concert.

By September the decision had been made to purchase a new President's badge bearing the correct logo and Choir name. As the calendar year progressed, John Christian again came to the assistance of the Secretary by setting up a new and much more professional website of nine pages. This in turn reaped much benefit for the Choir and new members were recruited through it. An analysis of the first few months showed it had seven thousand, eight hundred and sixteen 'hits'. A further professional look for the Choir came through the purchase of one hundred music folders bearing the Choir logo on the cover. The cost was £575 and a generous member of the Choir met £400 of this.

In March, 2009, after a lapse of many years, a Choir dinner was held at the Palace Hotel, Paignton. Although attended by only thirty-three members and their partners it proved to be an enjoyable experience with both the President and Director of Music and his wife attending. For the forthcoming March Mozart concert the Committee had already examined ways in which the sales might be increased for what was considered a popular concert. A local free newspaper was used for a distribution in specific targeted areas with five thousand leaflets being inserted in its pages. A one pound discount on each ticket was offered on production of the leaflet if shown at the door on the night. So much for ambitious plans – only one lady (and she would have come anyway) took advantage of the offer!

As the season came to an end, the Choir moved into a new field of music neglected for many years, when it presented a concert of Handel's 'little opera' *Acis & Galatea*. The soloists semi-acted their parts and some visual still-pictures of the story, prepared by Choir member Clive Richards, were projected onto the walls in Central Church, Torquay, and a baroque orchestra (despite some last-minute harmonium problems) all contributed to make this a successful venture.

The well-known composer, John Rutter, was featured in the December, 2009, concert which included one of his works especially written for young people, *The Mass of the Children*. Because of commitments for many schools with their own carol and Christmas events, difficulty was experienced in finding young people to participate. Finally a group from Launceston, the 'Mini Minstrels of Cornwall', was found and the Choir supplied a coach and tea for the young people and some parents accompanying them. Attempts were again made to obtain some free, pre-concert, publicity by an unusual method. As one of the pieces in the concert was *When Icicles Hang*, a small number of Choir singers descended into the bowels of Kent's Cavern. With the kind co-operation of the management, the Choir members would appear to be singing around the stalactites and stalagmites to 'get in the mood' for the concert. This was an interesting idea but unfortunately never made print probably because of pressure on space at that time of the year. Perhaps, in the end, extra publicity was not needed as over two hundred and twenty people filled the seats at the Central Church for this popular composer.

At the AGM in January, 2010, the Treasurer presented her accounts for the year ending 31 August, 2009, and indicated an almost novel situation in that the Choir was carrying forward a balance of £5,260. The Committee felt that if an application for funding was made, a benefactor might not consider a grant justified. However, this large sum had deliberately been built-up to cushion a large deficit anticipated for the next 3CD concert due in 2010. Concerns were also expressed at the AGM that the Choir was rather out-growing the space available at the rehearsal hall and at some of the venues for concerts. As an un-auditioned Choir, restrictions were considered in accepting further members but they were not implemented at this stage.

In September, 2009, the Plymouth & SW Co-operative Society merged into the national Co-operative Group which meant the last instalment of sponsorship, which the Choir had enjoyed since 1991, was stopped. The Choir would now have to make application under the Group's Community Development Fund for a project which would have to meet specified criteria. We are delighted that this book was just such a venture that they were able to support.

As Summer approached, yet again considerable background planning had taken place in previous months for the third triennial 3CD concert. On this occasion only two choirs would participate, as Stanborough Chorus had to withdraw because of their twenty-fifth anniversary full programme. Vaughan Williams' *A Sea Symphony* was chosen as the major work and the title for the concert would be the 'Maritime Proms'. It was decided that the second half would be devoted to a 'Last Night of the Proms' format with an added sea theme including HMS Pinafore extracts and Dyson's *Four Songs for Sailors*. The June concert in the Torquay Town Hall Assembly Rooms had a disappointing audience attendance of just over two hundred, but the Barnstaple Pannier Market event was more successful with an audience of over three hundred. The latter event was linked to the North Devon Festival and gained suitable publicity through literature sent out nationwide. The deficit this time was nearly £7,000 and was met by use of the two choirs' reserve funds mentioned earlier. To maintain the maritime theme a pledge had already been given to the Royal National Lifeboat Institute to donate money to extend the provision of Beach Lifeguard cover in the West-country. A sum of £1480 was donated from the joint concert accounts.

Choir numbers were still increasing and the Committee resorted to inserting a piece in the website stating: "we welcome tenor voices but, in order to give a balance we may have to restrict the number of other voice parts for the time being". However, new singers were still advised to contact the Secretary to ascertain the latest position regarding membership. The Committee certainly did not wish to deter new singers but, if necessary, a waiting-list might have to be built up. This problem was highlighted for the stage management team when the November concert at All Saints Church, Babbacombe, Torquay was being planned because of fixed Choir stalls and moving any congregation pews. The Church was chosen because of the very fine organ to be played by Christopher Sears in the concert and also because he was, and still is, Organist and Choirmaster. Again this concert contained works new to the Choir composed by Duruflé and Gounod.

New technology was extensively used for the Winter edition of 'Devon Musical Notes' (as it was now called and to which earlier references have been made), when electronic mail was used for the first time. Just under sixty societies were now contributing over the whole of Devon, and the failure to obtain continued funding for costs from local councils to produce the diary meant that this was the most effective way without placing a financial burden on Choir funds. It also had the advantage that it could reach a larger audience and some choirs were already mailing out a personal copy to all their members.

As 2011 progressed, the third 'Angela Barton Memorial' Spring concert included Mozart's *Requiem Mass in D minor*, a favourite work of the late Mrs Barton. For the Summer an operetta not performed since 1970, *Tom Jones*, was presented. With its West-country story and dialogue this was very appropriate and was enhanced again by still pictures of the story on the walls of Central Church.

As an aside it should be added here that on 16 July, 2011, after eighty-six years as a daily newspaper, the 'Herald Express' in Torbay became a weekly edition. It had been invaluable in publishing articles and occasional photographs of the Choir over that period and some of these appear in this book.

The Choir was particularly pleased to mark its 140th Anniversary by including in its concert in November, 2011, the same piece which had been performed at its first concert in 1878, Mendelssohn's *Hear my Prayer*. Several choral classics were added to another work by this composer, the *Hymn of Praise*, which occupied the major part of the 2011 programme. Five days later a Celebration Buffet was held at the Berry Head Hotel, Brixham. This gave the opportunity for past and present members, numbering one hundred and twelve, to share in some memories of both old and more recent times. A slide show of photographs over the years and supporting historical files containing cuttings, concert programmes, photographs and other memorabilia were also on display.

To end this final chapter and 2011, as the Choir had been the first choir to be included, it was invited to participate in the twenty-fifth anniversary of the Civic Carol Concert at the International Riviera Centre. Conducted by Dr Trevor Bray, and accompanied by Sue Merryweather, who had been the Choir's Accompanist from 1986 to 2000, the Choir presented four items of Christmas music to the large audience at the Centre. What a fitting end to one hundred and forty years of history for the Choir!

APPENDICES

(Pre 1946, because of the almost total reliance on newspaper articles which did not very often detail information about Annual General Meetings and other events, date accuracy has been difficult to record at times except in the Society/Choir section.)

HON CONDUCTORS/DIRECTORS OF MUSIC

Sep 1878 – Apr 1880	Mr Michael Rice
Oct 1885 – Jan 1886	Mr Frank Harris ⎫ Joint
	Mr Samuel Martin ⎬ Conductors
Jan 1886 – Feb 1888	Mr Frank Harris
Sep 1895 – Feb 1898	Mr Frank Harris
Jan 1905 – Jan 1906	Mr Frank Harris ⎫ Joint
	Mr Frank Benson ⎬ Conductors
Sep 1909?-Mar 1912	Mr Wilfred Layton
Sep 1920 – Dec 1920	Mr Frank Harris
Jan 1921 – Apr 1921	Mr Frank Benson
Oct 1921 – Oct 1927	Mr Herbert Rushton
Jul 1928 – Dec 1936	Mr Leonard Baggaley
Jan 1937 – Mar 1939	Mr Gerald King
Oct 1946 – Jan 1957	Dr A Fairburn Barnes
Sep 1957 – Oct 1957	Mr Derek Browning
Oct 1957 – Aug 1958	Mr Denis Isles
Oct 1958 – May 1961	Mr John Nancekevill
Jul 1961 – Dec 1965	Mr William Humpherson
Jan 1966 – May 1966	Mr Bruce Ferris
Sep 1966 – Aug 1973	Mr Archibald Marcom
Sep 1973 – Aug 1982	Mr Fred Duerden
Sep 1982 – Aug 1986	Mr Howard Hoar
Sep 1986 – Mar 2007	Mr Melvyn Batten
Sep 2007 – to date	Mr John Hobbs

PRESIDENTS

Sep 1878 - ?	Dr Charles Pridham
Jan 1905 - ?	Rev Dr John Trelawny-Ross

(Presidents of the Paignton Musical Association which included the Choral Section)

Jan1919 - ?	Mr Arthur James
Sep 1923 – May 1931	Rev H Mackworth Drake
Jun 1931 - ?	Mr Geoffrey Spanton
Jan 1937 - ?	Rev Basil Drake

(Presidents of the Paignton, Operatic, Dramatic and Choral Society)

Nov 1947 - ?	Mr J. Huggins
1972 – Feb 1982	Mr William Loates

(Paignton Choral Society)

Dec 1982 – Jun 1983	Mr Norman Del Mar
Mar 2000 – Apr 2007	Mr Vince McCann
Jan 2008 – to date	Mr Mike Thompson

CHAIRPERSONS

Sep 1895 – Sep 1896	Dr James Alexander
Oct 1896 – Feb 1878	Mr William Goodale
Jan 1905? – Jan 1907 ?	Mr Archibald Spens
Sep 1920 – Aug 1921	Mr Robert Waycott
Sep 1920 - ?	Mr H. Higgs
Oct 1946 – Sep 1947	Mr Alexander McMannes
Oct 1947 – Aug 1948	Mr William Bourne
Oct 1948 – Sep 1950	Mr Eddie Harris
Oct 1950 – May 1951	Mr Lesley Quarrell
May 1951 – Aug 1952	Mr E. Davies
Sep 1952 – Apr 1953	Mrs Gladys Williams
May 1953 – Apr 1964	Mr Fred Forrester
May 1964 – ?	Mr Herbert Haddon
Sep 1965 – Aug 1966	Mr Eddie Harris
Sep 1966 – Aug 1970	Mr Fred Forrester
Sep 1970 – May 1972	Mr Howard Leaman
May 1972 – Aug 1974	Mr Eddie Thomas
Sep 1974 – Aug 1976	Mr Mike Griffiths
Sep 1976 – Dec 1977	Mr George Harris
Jan 1977 – Aug 1978	Mr Eddie Thomas
Sep 1978 – Aug 1980	Mr Mike Griffths
Sep 1980 – Aug 1982	Mr Les Ayres
Sep 1982 – Aug 1986	Miss Helen Tregaskes
Sep 1986 – Aug 1988	Mr Wilf Forrester
Sep 1988 – Aug 1995	Mrs Prim Wood
Sep 1995 – Aug 1999	Dr David Taylor
Sep 1999 - Aug 2001	Mr Adrian Mansfield
Sep 2001 – to date	Mrs Pat Wyatt

SOCIETY/CHOIR CONCERTS

(Note, only the choral items performed in any concert are shown here. The programme may have included other orchestral, organ or piano pieces. Individual carols performed at Christmas concerts are not shown. In the very early dates, a number of solos or part pieces were included in a concert given by guest artistes or a group of members in the Society. These are also not recorded.)

Venues. Many appear frequently – the locations of which are shown below. Other venues are specifically detailed: Public Hall (later Palace Avenue Theatre), Palace Avenue, Paignton; Palace Avenue Methodist Church, Palace Avenue, Paignton; Christ Church, Lower Polsham Road, Paignton; Festival Theatre, The Esplanade, Paignton; Central Church, Tor Hill Road, Torquay; All Saints Church, Cary Park, Babbacombe, Torquay.

Date	Venue	Concert Programme
1800		
13.12.78	The Arena, Oldway	Mendelssohn *Hear my prayer; Happy Lovers*; *Shepherd's song*; (?) *The Vikings* (?) *Who shall Win my love*;
22.10.79	Bijou Theatre Torbay Road, Paignton	Cowen *The Rose Maiden* Mendelssohn *The Vikings*
7.1.80	Bijou Theatre Torbay Road, Paignton	Rossini *Hark how the horns (William Tell)*; Auber *The Market Chorus (Masaniello)* (?) *Sir Knight! Sir Knight* (?) *Little Jack Horner*; (?) *Good night*
7.4.80	Bijou Theatre Torbay Road Paignton	Spohr *God Thou are great;* Mendelssohn *Hear my prayer;* Gade *The Erl King's daughter*
27.1.86	Temperance Hall New Street, Paignton	Anderton *Wreck of the Hesperus;* Cowen *Bridal Chorus (The Rose Maiden);* Danby *Awake Aeolian Lyre*
19.5.86	Temperance Hall New Street, Paignton	Romberg *The Lay of the Bell;* Schumann *Gypsy Life;* Mendelssohn *I would that my love;* Löhr *A Border Raid*
20.1.87	Temperance Hall New Street, Paignton	Bennett *May Queen*
1.6.87	Temperance Hall New Street, Paignton	Handel *Judas Maccabaeus*
14.4.96	Public Hall	Mendelssohn *Hymn of Praise & Let all men praise the Lord*; Wagner *The spinning chorus (Flying Dutchman);* (?) *Down in a flowr'y vale*
11.1.97	Public Hall	Iliffe *Morning*; Weber *The soft winds (Preciosa)*; (?) *The chough and the crow*; (?) *A song of Spring*

109

Date	Venue	Concert Programme
1900		
11.4.05	Public Hall	Mendelssohn *Athalie*;
		Haydn *The heavens are telling (The Creation)*
8.12.09	Public Hall	Mendelssohn *Hymn of Praise* (Part II)
		Haydn *The Creation* (Part II);
9.3.10	Public Hall	Beethoven *Choral Fantasia*;
		Sullivan *The evening hymn (A Golden Legend)*;
		Elgar *The Snow*
14.12.10	Public Hall	Brahms *A song of destiny* Mendelssohn *Lorely*
29.3.11	Public Hall	Handel *Messiah* (Part II); Gounod *Gallia*
13.12.11	Public Hall	Coleridge-Taylor *Hiawatha's Wedding Feast*
		& Death of Minnehaha
27.3.12	Public Hall	Schubert *Song of Miriam;*
		Bach *God so loved the world*
14.12.20	Public Hall	Bennett *May Queen* Shaw *A New Year's carol*
13.4.21	Public Hall	Coleridge-Taylor *Hiawatha's Wedding Feast*
8.1.22	Public Hall	Coleridge-Taylor *Hiawatha's The Departure;*
		Rhodes *The Voices of Spring*
12.12.22	Public Hall	German *Tom Jones*
2.5.23	Public Hall	Haydn *The Creation* (Parts I & II);
		Rhodes *I would I were a glow-worm*
12.12.23	Public Hall	Gaul *Joan of Arc*
4.4.25	Public Hall	Mendelssohn *Elijah*
27.3.26	Public Hall	Handel *Messiah*
26.5.37	Public Hall	Handel *Messiah*
27.4.38	Public Hall	Coleridge-Taylor *Bon Bon Suite* Gounod *Soldiers'*
		Chorus (Faust)
1.3.39	Public Hall	Mendelssohn *Elijah*
30.11.46	St Andrew's Church	Mendelssohn *Lauda Sion*
	Sands Road, Paignton	Barnes *Our fathers to their graves have gone*
30.4.47	Public Hall	Elgar *Scenes from the Bavarian Highlands*
		Wagner *Choral Fantasia (Tannhaüser)*
29.11.47	St Andrew's Church	Handel *Messiah*
	Sands Road, Paignton	
4&5.5.48	Public Hall	Coleridge-Taylor *Hiawatha's Wedding Feast*
		& The Death of Minnehaha
4.12.48	Public Hall	Mendelssohn *Elijah*
2.4.49	Palace Avenue Th	Elgar *The Banner of St George;*
		Parry *Blest Pair of Sirens*
7&8.12.49	Palace Avenue Th	German *Merrie England*
23.3.50	Palace Avenue	Handel *Messiah* (excerpts)
	Methodist Church	Bach *Praise the Lord*
13.12.50	Christ Church	Concert of anthems & carols
29.11.51	Palace Avenue Th	Coleridge-Taylor *Hiawatha's Wedding Feast*
		& The Death of Minnehaha
27.3.52	Palace Avenue Th	Mendelssohn *Elijah* (excerpts); *13th Psalm*
	Methodist Church	

Date	Venue	Concert Programme
4.12.52	Parish Hall, Paignton	Carol concert
26.1.53	Christ Church	Choral concert
19.3.53	Palace Avenue Methodist Church	Handel *Messiah* (excerpts)
9.12.53	Palace Avenue Methodist Church	Handel *Messiah*
31.3.54	Palace Avenue Th	Phillips *The Rebel Maid*
1.12.54	Palace Avenue Methodist Church	Christmas concert including Handel *Hallelujah Chorus (Messiah)* & Mendelssohn *Lauda Sion*
5.10.55	Badminton Hall Paignton	Stanford *Songs of the Fleet* & *The Revenge*
25.4.56	Palace Avenue Th	Haydn *The Creation*
28.11.56	Palace Avenue Methodist Church	Handel *Messiah* (excerpts) & carols
15.5.57	Palace Avenue Th	Coleridge-Taylor *Hiawatha's Wedding Feast* & *Death of Minnehaha*
11.12.57	Palace Avenue Th	V Williams *Fantasia on Christmas Carols* Bach *Christmas Oratorio* (Parts I & II)
30.4.58	Palace Avenue Th	Bizet *Carmen* (concert version)
10.12.58	Palace Avenue Methodist Church	Handel *Messiah* (part I) with Christmas music
20.5.59	Christ Church	Handel *Judas Maccabaeus*
21.5.59	St Luke's Church Sheddon Hill, Torquay	As above
3.12.59	Christ Church	Handel *Messiah*
25.5.60	Christ Church	Mendelssohn *Elijah*
24.11.60	Christ Church	Mendelssohn *Hymn of Praise* Bach *Sleepers Awake*; V Williams *Old 100th*
6.12.61	Christ Church	Handel *Messiah* (excerpts) V Williams *Fantasia on Christmas Carols* Britten *Rejoice in the Lamb*
9.5.62	Christ Church	Haydn *Imperial Mass*; Green *Lord let me know mine end*; Mendelssohn *Hear my prayer*; Bach *Jesu, Joy of man's desiring* V Williams *O, clap your hands*
5.12.62	Palace Avenue Methodist Church	Bach *Christmas Oratorio* & carols
1.5.63	Palace Avenue Th	Haydn *The Seasons*
11.12.63	Christ Church	Handel *Messiah*
13.5.64	St Paul's Church Preston, Paignton	Britten *St Nicolas* Bach *Jesu, Priceless Treasure*
10.12.64	Palace Avenue Methodist Church	Schütz *Christmas Oratorio* with carols
7.4.65	Christ Church	Mendelssohn *Elijah*
9.12.65	Palace Avenue Methodist Church	V Williams *Fantasia on Christmas Carols* Britten *Rejoice in the Lamb*

111

Date	Venue	Concert Programme
14.12.66	Palace Avenue Methodist Church	Handel *Messiah* (excerpts) and carols
12.4.67	Christ Church	Haydn *The Creation*
2.11.67	St John's Church Strand, Torquay	As above
28&29.11.67	Palace Avenue Th	Strauss *The Blue Danube* Weber *Invitation to the Dance* & *Holy Child*; Thiman *Gloria in excelsis Deo*
1.5.68	Palace Avenue Th	Coleridge-Taylor *Hiawatha's Wedding Feast* & *The Death of Minnehaha*
10.12.68	Christ Church	Brahms *German Requiem;* Mendelssohn *Hear my prayer*
23.4.69	Palace Avenue Th	German *Merrie England*
11.12.69	Palace Avenue Methodist Church	Bush *In Praise of Mary* & carols
15.4.70	Palace Avenue Th	German *Tom Jones*
9.12.70	Christ Church	Thiman *The Nativity* Handel *Messiah* (excerpts) & carols
27.3.71	Festival Theatre	Handel *Messiah*
8.12.71	Christ Church	Handel *Messiah* (excerpts); Cashmore *This child behold* & Christmas music
18.3.72	Festival Theatre	Mendelssohn *Elijah*
6.12.72	Christ Church	Bach *Christmas Oratorio* (parts I & II); Handel *Messiah* (excerpts) & Christmas music
7.4.73	Festival Theatre	Bach *St Matthew Passion*
15.12.73	Christ Church	Handel *Messiah*
4.5.74	Festival Theatre	Gilbert & Sullivan (excerpts from *Mikado)*; *Gondoliers; Pirates of Penzance*
7.12.74	Christ Church	Handel *Messiah* (excerpts) & carols
22.5.75	Christ Church	Brahms *German Requiem*; Parry *Jerusalem*; Mendelssohn *Hear my prayer;* Mozart *Ave verum Corpus*
13.12.75	Festival Theatre	Carol concert
20.5.76	Christ Church	Vivaldi *Gloria*; V Williams *Benedicite*; Mozart *Laudate Pueri*; Handel *Zadok the Priest*
11.12.76	Festival Theatre	Handel *Messiah* (excerpts) & carols
19.5.77	Christ Church	Haydn *The Creation*; Parry *Jersualem*; Elgar *Pomp & Circumstance No 1;* V Williams *Old 100th*
10.12.77	Festival Theatre	Carol concert
18.5.78	Christ Church	Dvořák *Stabat Mater;* V Williams *Towards the Unknown Region*
16.12.78	Festival Theatre	Carol concert
10.5.79	Christ Church	Mozart *Requiem Mass* Mendelssohn *Hymn of praise*
18.11.79	Festival Theatre	Brahms *German Requiem*

112

Date	Venue	Concert Programme
8.12.79	Festival Theatre	Handel Messiah (excerpts) & carols
20.3.80	Festival Theatre	Handel *Messiah*
13.12.80	Festival Theatre	Handel Messiah (excerpts) & carols
21.12.80	Festival Theatre	Carol concert
14.5.81	Paignton Parish Church	Vivaldi *Gloria*; Haydn *Imperial Nelson Mass*
12.11.81	Christ Church	Verdi *Grand Chorus (Aida)*; Handel *Let their Celestial Concerts*; Parry *I was glad*; Strauss *Waltz (Die Fledermaus)*; Quilter *Non Nobis, Domine*; Shaw *Amazing Grace*; Sullivan *The long day closes*; Mendelssohn. *As the hart pants*; Mozart *Glorious is Thy Name*; Elgar *Pomp & Circumstance No 1* plus negro spirituals
5.12.81	Palace Avenue Th	Carol concert
20.5.82	Christ Church	Mendelssohn *Come let us sing*; Mozart *First Mass in C*; Mendelssohn *As the hart pants*
2.12.82	Christ Church	Bach *Christmas Oratorio* Handel *Messiah* (excerpts) & carols
18.5.83	Paignton Parish Church	Mendelssohn *Elijah*
19.5.83	St Paul's Church Preston, Paignton	As above
17.11.83	St Paul's Church	Haydn *The Creation*
10.12.83	Festival Theatre	Handel Messiah (excerpts) & carols
16.5.84	St Paul's Church Preston, Paignton	Fauré *Requiem*; Handel *Samson* (excerpts)
17.5.84	Christ Church	As above
22.11.84	St Paul's Church	Mendelssohn *St Paul*
15.12.84	Festival Theatre	Carol concert
3.4.85	St Paul's Church Paignton	Bach *St Matthew Passion* (excerpts)
23.5.85	Christ Church	Handel *Judas Maccabaeus*
7.11.85	St Paul's Church Paignton	Mendelssohn *Hymn of Praise*; Verdi *Grand March (Aida)*; Parry *I was glad*; Williams *Trade Winds*; Sullivan *The long day closes*; Handel *O praise the Lord.*
14.12.85	Festival Theatre	Carol concert
25.3.86	Winner Street Baptist Church	Maunder *Olivet to Calvary*
26.3.86	United Reformed Church, Paignton	As above
22.5.86	Central Church	Bach *Magnificat in D;* Elgar *Scenes from The Bavarian Highlands*; Rossini *Stabat Mater*
15.11.86	Central Church	Handel *Zadok the Priest*; Britten *St Nicolas*
6.12.86	Festival Theatre	Handel *Messiah* (excerpts) & carols
2.5.87	Central Church	Orff *Carmina Burana*

Date	Venue	Concert Programme
14.11.87	Central Church	Handel *Messiah*
12.12.87	Festival Theatre	Carol concert
12.3.88	Central Church	Kodaly *Missa Brevis*; Rossini *Petite Messe Solennelle*
25.6.88	Central Church	Elgar *Dream of Gerontius*
12.11.88	Central Church	Mozart *Requiem Mass*
3.12.88	Festival Theatre	Carol concert
11.3.89	Central Church	Rutter *Requiem*; Byrt *Exaudi Domini*
10.6.89	Central Church	Berlioz *Te Deum*; Kodaly *Te Deum*
11.6.89	St Peter's Church, Ilfracombe	As above
17.8.89	St Corentin Cathedral Quimper, France	As above
11.11.89	Central Church	Mendelssohn *Elijah*
2.12.89	Central Church	Handel *Messiah*
10.3.90	Central Church	Beethoven *Choral Fantasia* & *Mass in C*
9.6.90	English Riviera Centre, Torquay	V Williams *A Sea Symphony*
10.8.90	St Corentin Cathedral Quimper, France	Beethoven *Missa Solemnis*
11.8.90	St Mathieu Church Quimper, France	Bach *Mass in C*
10.11.90	Central Church	Elgar *The Music Makers*; Lambert *Rio Grande*
1.12.90	Central Church	Handel *Messiah*
9.3.91	St Luke's Church, Torquay	Vivaldi *Gloria in D*; Stanford *Heraclitus;* Anon *Rejoice in the Lord alway*
11.5.91	Central Church	Fauré *Cantique de Jean Racine*; Quilter *Non Nobis Domine*; Handel *Messiah* (excerpts)
30.6.91	Festival Theatre	Verdi *Requiem*
16.11.91	Central Church	Beethoven *Mass in D (Missa Solemnis)*
7.12.91	Central Church	Carol concert
8.12.91	St Mary's Church, Brixham	Carol concert
14.3.92	St Luke's Church, Torquay	Stainer *Crucifixion*; Fauré *Requiem*
27.6.92	English Riviera Centre, Torquay	Orff *Carmina Burana*; Verdi *Chorus of Hebrew Slaves*; Lehar *Merry Widow* (excerpts); Strauss *Nuns' Chorus*
17.11.92	Exeter Cathedral	Elgar *The Dream of Gerontius*
5.12.92	Central Church	Carol concert
27.3.93	Central Church	Walton *Coronation Te Deum*; V Williams *Old 100th*; Parry *I was glad* & *Jerusalem*; Handel *Zadok The Priest*; Elgar *Pomp & Circumstance March No 1*
1.6.93	All Saints Church, Brixham	V Williams *The old 100th* & *Let all the world*; Parry *I was glad* & *Jerusalem*; Handel *Zadok*

Date	Venue	Concert Programme
		the Priest; Stanford *Magnificat & Nunc Dimittis*; Bairstow *Save us O Lord*; Rutter *A Gaelic Blessing*; Lyte *Abide with me*
26.6.93	Village Hall, Abbotskerswell	As above (excluding Lyte) including Bizet *Carmen* (excerpts)
20.11.93	Central Church	Haydn *Nelson Mass*; Britten *St Nicolas*
23.11.93	St Mary's Church	Haydn *Nelson Mass*
12.12.93	Festival Theatre	Carol concert
26.3.94	Torquay Town Hall	Brahms *German Requiem*
18.6.94	Village Hall	V Williams *Towards the unknown region*; Borodin *Polovtsian Dances*; G&S *Pirates of Penzance*; Schönberg *Les Misérables*.
25.6.94	Torquay Town Hall	As above
26.11.94	St Mary the Virgin Parish Church, Torquay	Haydn *The Creation*
17.12.94	Torquay Town Hall	Carol concert
25.3.95	St Luke's Church, Torquay	Bach *St John Passion*
24.6.95	Central Church	Walton *Belshazzar's Feast*
19.11.95	Torquay Town Hall	Mendelssohn *Elijah*
30.3.96	St Mary the Virgin Parish Church, Torquay	Wood *Hail gladdening light*; Rutter *Requiem*
22.6.96	Riviera Centre	Verdi *Requiem*
24.11.96	Torquay Town Hall	Handel *Messiah*
15.3.97	St Mary the Virgin	Puccini *Messa di Gloria*; Skempton *Two poems of Edward Thomas*
21.6.97	Festival Theatre	Dyson *Canterbury Pilgrims*
18.10.97	Festival Theatre	Handel *Messiah*
7.12.97	Torquay Town Hall	Carol concert
10.4.98	Christ Church	Stainer *The Crucifixion*
9.5.98	Torquay Town Hall	Elgar *The Dream of Gerontius*
18.7.98	Hall for Cornwall, Truro	Orff *Carmina Burana*; Lambert *Rio Grande*
14.11.98	Central Church	Beethoven *Mass in C major* & *A Calm Sea*
6.12.98	Torquay Town Hall	Carol concert incl Rutter *Brother Heinrich Christmas*
27.3.99	St Mary's Church Abbotsbury, N Abbot	Vivaldi *Gloria*; Pitoni *Cantate Domino* Correa *O vos Omnes*; Rutter *Praise ye the Lord*
2.5.99	Church of St Peter, Caen	Vivaldi *Gloria* (excerpts)
3.5.99	Church on the outskirts of Caen	Vivaldi *Gloria*
12.6.99	Central Church	V Williams *A Cotswold Romance*; Verdi *Chorus of Hebrew Slaves*; Puccini *Humming Chorus*; Mascagni *The Easter Hymn*
13.11.99	Central Church	Brahms *German Requiem*
12.12.99	All Saints Church	Carol concert

Date	Venue	Concert Programme

2000

Date	Venue	Concert Programme
21.4.00	Christ Church	Fauré *Requiem* & *Cantique de Jean Racine;* Edwards *Immortality*
9.7.00	Torquay Town Hall	Berlioz *Te Deum*; Leedham *Fanfare for the New Millennium*
14.10.00	Central Church	Handel *Messiah*
28.10.00	St Nazaire Church, France	Berlioz *Te Deum*
9.12.00	Central Church	Mozart *Requiem in D minor*
31.3.01	Central Church	Elgar *The music makers* & *Blest pair of Sirens*
7.7.01	Central Church	Excerpts from: Wagner *Processional Chorus (Meistersinger* & *Bridal Chorus (Lohengrin)*; Bizet *Carmen* (excerpts); Carter *Benedicite*
10.11.01	Central Church	Haydn *The Creation*
14.12.01	St Mary's Church, Abbotsbury, N Abbot	Carol concert
29.3.02	St Mary the Virgin Parish Church, Torquay	Dvořák *Stabat Mater*
13.6.02	All Saints Church	V Williams *Old 100th*; Parry *I was glad*; Wesley *Thou wilt keep him*; V Williams *O taste and see*; Purcell *Thou knowest*; Brahms *How lovely are Thy dwellings*; Handel *Zadok the Priest* & *The King shall rejoice*
24.11.02	Torquay Town Hall	Mendelssohn *Elijah*
1.3.03	Central Church	Wood *Hail gladdening light*; Rutter *For the beauty* & *I will lift up mine eyes* & *The Lord bless you* & *Requiem*
17.5.03	Central Church	Praetorius *Viva la musica*; Boyce *Alleluia*; Thompson *Alleluia;* Vincert *Dream world*; Vivaldi *Gloria in D major*
15.11.03	Central Church	Schubert *Psalm 23* & *Mass in F*
20.3.04	Torquay Town Hall	Verdi *Requiem*
21.3.04	Barnstaple Pannier Market	As above
10.6.04	All Saints Church	Britten *O sing joyfully*; Mozart Ave *Verum Corpus*; Franck *Panis Angelicus*; Mendelssohn *Hear my prayer*; Stainer *God so loved the world*; Fauré *Cantique de Jean Racine*; Elgar *Give unto the Lord*; Parry *I was glad*; Bruckner *Locus Iste*; Brahms *How lovely are Thy dwellings*; Schubert *Sanctus*; Britten *Hymn to the Virgin*; Bach-Gounod *Ave Maria*; Handel *Zadok the Priest*
13.11.04	Central Church	Poulenc *Gloria*; Fauré *Cantique de Jean Racine*; Britten *St Nicolas*
25.3.05	All Saints Church	Handel *Messiah* (part II); Stainer *Crucifxion*

116

Date	Venue	Concert Programme
30.4.05	Central Church	V Williams *A Sea Symphony* & *Five mystical songs*
14.5.05	Ripon Cathedral	V Williams *A Sea Symphony*
25.6.05	All Saints Church	Stanford *Te Deum Laudamus*; Elgar *Ave Verum Corpus*; Mendelssohn *Hear my prayer*; Bach *Jesu joy of man's desiring*; V Williams *Let all the world*; Schubert *Mass in G*
26.11.05	Central Church	Puccini *Messa di Gloria*; Donizetti *Chorus of the wedding guests (Lucia di Lammermoor)*; Verdi *Chorus of the Hebrew slaves (Nabucco)*; Puccini *Humming Chorus (Madame Butterfly)*; Verdi *Anvil Chorus (Il Trovatore)*; Mascagni *Easter Hymn (Cavalleria Rusticana)*
1.4.06	Central Church	Elgar *Dream of Gerontius*
1.7.06	Central Church	Dvořák *Mass in D*
18.11.06	Central Church	Brahms *German Requiem*
12.12.06	Riviera Centre, Torquay	Civic carol concert
17.3.07	Central Church	Handel *Messiah*
19.5.07	Torquay Town Hall	Orff *Carmina Burana*; Mendelssohn *Die Erste Walpurgisnacht*
20.5.07	Barnstaple Pannier Market	as above
16.12.07	All Saints Church, Brixham	Bach *Christmas Oratorio*
5.4.08	Central Church	Cherubini *Requiem*; Puccini *Messa di Gloria*
12.7.08	Central Church	Elgar *Scenes from the Bavarian Highlands*; Parry *Pied Piper of Hamelin*; Coleridge-Taylor *Hiawatha's Wedding Feast*
29.11.08	Christ Church	Bizet *Te Deum*; Charpentier *Messe de Minuit pour Noël*; Saint Saëns *Christmas Oratorio*
28.3.09	Central Church	Mozart *Mass in C minor*; Haydn *Nelson Imperial Mass*
13.6.09	Central Church	Handel *Acis & Galatea*
5.12.09	Central Church	Rutter *Mass of the children* & *When icicles hang* & *Feel the Spirit*
27.3.10	Christ Church	Rossini *Stabat Mater*; Fauré *Requiem* & *Cantique de Jean Racine*
19.6.10	Torquay Town Hall	V Williams *A Sea Symphony*; Dyson *Four songs for sailors*; Wood *Fantasia on British sea songs*; Parry *Jerusalem*; Elgar *Pomp & Circumstance No 1*
20.6.10	Barnstaple Pannier Market	As above
27.11.10	All Saints Church, Torquay	Duruflé *Requiem*; Gounod *Messe Solennelle St Cecilia*
16.4.11	Central Church	Mozart *Vespers Solennelles de Confessore* & *Ave Verum Corpus* & *Requiem in D minor*
2.7.11	Central Church	German *Tom Jones*

Date	Venue	Concert Programme
26.11.11	Central Church	Mendelssohn *Hymn of Praise* & *Hear my prayer*; Haydn *Insanae et Vanae Curae*; Brahms *How lovely are Thy dwellings*; Elgar *Give unto the Lord*; Parry *Blest pair of Sirens*